The Academic Library Building in the Digital Age: A Study of Construction, Planning, and Design of New Library Space

by Christopher Stewart

Association of College and Research Libraries
A division of the American Library Association
Chicago, Illinois 2010

The paper used in this publication meets the minimum requirements of American National Standard for Information Sciences–Permanence of Paper for Printed Library Materials, ANSI Z39.48-1992. ∞

Library of Congress Cataloging-in-Publication Data

Stewart, Christopher, 1966 Feb. 4-
The academic library building in the digital age : a study of construction, planning, and design of new library space / Christopher Stewart.
p. cm.
Includes bibliographical references.
ISBN 978-0-8389-8552-6 (pbk. : alk. paper) 1. Library buildings--United States--Design and construction. 2. Library buildings--United States--Territories and possessions--Design and construction. 3. Library buildings--United States--Planning. 4. Library buildings--United States--Territories and possessions--Planning. 5. Academic libraries--Space utilization--United States. 6. Academic libraries--Space utilization--United States--Territories and possessions. 7. Library architecture--United States. 8. Library architecture--United States--Territories and possessions. 9. Library surveys--United States. 10. Library surveys--United States--Territories and possessions. I. Title.
Z679.2.U54S74 2010
727'.80973--dc22

2010024659

Printed in the United States of America.

14 13 12 11 10   5 4 3 2 1

Table of Contents

chapter one

WHY STUDY ACADEMIC LIBRARY BUILDINGS?

A Changing Landscape

Few quarters in higher education have changed as dramatically over the past few decades as the academic library. Digitization and the ubiquitous, unmediated nature of information in a networked environment have altered models for delivering scholarly information and reinforced perceptions of the library's diminishing importance as a physical space (Carlson, 2001). Meanwhile, the library's ability to ensure information literacy, provide space conducive to collaboration and learning, and satisfy faculty demands for collections across a range of disciplines and formats is compromised by increased competition for institutional resources.

At the flashpoint of this change is the library building. At many colleges and universities, the library building is located at the heart of the campus. It serves as a powerful symbol of academic life and is often one of the largest facilities on campus. While ever-evolving information technologies have caused speculation about the future of the library building for decades (Dowler, 1996), the preponderance of the Internet has fueled much of the current debate about the role of the library building in modern academic life. In the 1990s, it was believed that the Internet's implications for transforming information delivery threatened libraries. This perception resulted in a "siege mentality," and speculation that, as the dominance of print waned, the library building itself would disappear (Demas, 2005). As the dust settled, however, new academic libraries continued to be built. In the period 1995-2002, more than 350 academic library construction projects, renovations, and additions were completed in the United States (Shill & Tonner, 2003). The study you will read about in the following pages picks up where research on new academic library buildings left off in the early part of this decade. In doing so, it is the first comprehensive study of planning and construction of academic library buildings completed entirely in the new century.

Background

During much of the 20th century, as physical collections grew, the focus of the academic library was its function as a repository for expanding collections across ever widening disciplines and specialized subjects. The modern American academic library's growth has paralleled that of higher education in general. With curricular reforms of the mid-late 19th century and the rise of the modern research university, the library's role as the center of university life and a powerful symbol of intellectual strength was unrivaled (Atkins, 1991). The emergence of the applied arts, the growth of American publishing, and the onset of curricular reforms that were to continue in the coming decades quickened the pace of the academic library's transformation as an increasingly vital part of the university, particularly library print collections. The unprecedented growth of American higher education in the decades after World War II marked another period of expansion for the academic and research library. By the late 20th century, the academic library had become an extremely cramped space, with swelling book collections crowding out user space (Freeman, 2005). The library had become a dry, "technical" place (Demas, 2005, p. 25). One library architect described these structures as "static buildings" that were "those we've inherited and are not those of the future" (Freeman, 2005, p. 1).

Today, most would agree that the academic library is in a period of ongoing transformation in the services it provides, the collections it offers, and the space it occupies. In this environment, one may expect to find change, perhaps even dramatic change, as technology, new modes of learning, and the shift from print to digital formats continue to transform higher education. For example, one may expect the new academic library space to illustrate the shift from a teaching-based enterprise to a learning-based enterprise, particularly, for example, the creation of collaborative spaces that emphasize the social dimensions of learning and knowledge (Bennett, 2003). While emerging frameworks for educational architecture (Monahan, 2002; Chism, 2006) are informing modern library design, new libraries must also continue to incorporate those traditional library values that remain as important for today's scholars as they have been for generations. Two important manifestations of these values are the library as a contemplative space for study and the library as a contemplative place for discovery—including the discovery of books.

Given digitization of collections, the dynamic mix of new learning spaces with traditional library functions, and other factors informing contemporary library design, the digital age has not raised so much the question of *if* libraries will survive, but *how* they will survive. To answer this question, one must look to academic library building projects completed in recent years.

Purpose and Significance of this Study

The general purpose of this study is to investigate the building of new academic libraries in the current era. In doing so, this study investigates levels of investment made by higher education in new library buildings, and how the changing role and purpose of the academic library is reflected in these buildings' planning, design, and use. This study builds in part on two earlier studies that examined academic library building and renovation projects completed primarily in the 1990s and early 2000s. The first study was a survey of academic library planning practices from 1992 to 2001, commissioned by the Council of Library and Information Resources (Bennett, 2003). The second study was conducted by academic librarians Hal Shill and Shawn Tonner and provided empirical data on building characteristics and post project usage on academic library projects completed between 1995 and 2002 (Shill & Tonner, 2003).

This new study includes all newly constructed academic library buildings in the United States and its territories completed in the seven-year period spanning 2003 through the end of 2009. This study is divided into two parts. The first part of the study was the creation of an inventory of all known, new academic library buildings in the United States completed between 2003 and 2009. This process of identifying and analyzing the population includes an analysis of academic library construction over this seven-year period across a several project variables (e.g., overall library building project cost and building cost per student), types of colleges and universities that completed new library buildings, and other institutional factors. This portion of the study also outlines the relationships between new academic library building projects and a range of institutional characteristics such as governance, enrollment profile, and institutional setting.

The second part of this study is a more in-depth investigation of these new library facilities through a detailed survey sent to each institution that completed a new library building. This survey asked library leaders at each institution for data on planning factors for the new library, characteristics of the new space, and usage. While the first part of the study identifies the number of library buildings constructed, at what size and cost, and at what types of institutions, the second part of the study explores what is happening *inside* these new libraries. Results from the survey provide information on factors that have informed the design of these libraries, including detailed data on new as well as traditional aspects of the academic library being included in these spaces. Finally, the survey portion of the study explores ways in which these new academic library buildings are being used.

In their study of new academic library building projects between 1995 and 2002, Shill and Tonner explained that one of the motivating factors for their work was the lack of empirical evidence linking library facility improvements and use. One of the goals of this study was to extend and expand data on library building projects by resuming the inquiry where Shill and Tonner and others left off in 2002, thereby adding significantly to the emerging body of knowledge on academic library planning and construction in the current era. By focusing on a population of new library buildings only, not renovations, however, this study differs from earlier studies in that it eliminates variables related to existing space, as is often the case with building additions and renovations. Results include data only from facilities planned and constructed entirely in the new century, and nearly a decade past the onset of the Internet era in the mid-1990s. Variables have been removed that, while relevant in earlier studies, are extraneous in the current study, including, for example, factors related to technology that are no longer complex and, for the most part, have been resolved in current building design. Evidence of the inclusion of traditional library spaces with social, collaborative, and public spaces is explored to determine how successful new libraries are at meeting evolving patron needs for the "development of separate spaces with specific characteristics" (Peterson, 2005, p. 59). A significant section of the survey investigates the relationship between modern building design and the growth of print and digital collections. Finally, by analyzing results against Carnegie classifications and data from the National Center for Educational Statistics, the survey describes relationships between library characteristics and design and specific kinds of institutions.

In his study of academic library planning factors, Bennett (2003) argues that library planning should be collaborative and move away from narrowly defined library standards such as seats and books. Space, he argues, should not be designed around supposed needs without asking how the library adds value to the educational experience. While much library planning well accommodates the role of the building as a research facility for access and preservation of collections, more focus in library design should be placed on teaching and learning functions of higher education and the library's role therein (Bennett, 2003). By asking a set of questions related to library planning similar to those that Bennett posed in his study of construction and renovation projects completed between 1992 and 2001, this study tests Bennett's observations on the limitations of library planning in the modern era and seeks to answer what, if any, lessons have been applied in libraries planned and constructed more recently.

By examining new academic library buildings completed between 2003 and 2009, the amount of available data on academic library planning and construction are extended by an additional seven years. Identifying academic library buildings completed between 2003 and 2009 informs an analysis of academic library building projects that will be useful for those tasked with making planning decisions about new academic library buildings. This analysis provides basic data on the number, cost, types of institutions building new libraries, and size of academic libraries completed over the past six years. Equally important, this analysis also compares library construction activity in the current era to that of the seven-year period immediately prior to the current era: 1996-2002. These data allow those involved in making decisions about building new academic libraries to assess general trends in library construction (beginning with, of course, information on whether academic library building activity has risen or declined) across a longer time frame and a larger study subset. Conclusions from this study can support future decision-making by providing university and library leaders and their planners with comprehensive information as to how, where, and why new libraries are being built, as well as how these new buildings are being used. This study should also be useful to researchers and others interested in the role of the building in the modern academic library mission. Finally, despite a subset limited to new library buildings at four-year and above institutions (previous studies included library renovations and community colleges), this study provides detailed information that describes current and emerging general trends in new library building design. It is hoped that the information presented here will also be useful for those planning significant renovations or, in general, library practitioners who are exploring better ways of using existing space.

Questions for the Research

Five primary research questions frame this study. The first two questions apply to the first portion of the study and rely on publicly available data for the academic library buildings completed between 2003 and 2009. The latter three questions are addressed in the second part of the study: the survey sent to library leaders at each institution that built a new library between 2003 and 2009. For institutions that built more than one new library during that period, a separate survey was sent for each building. The research questions are as follows:

1. For four-year colleges and universities, how does the current period of academic library construction compare to the previous period (1996–2002). Has the pace of library building construction accelerated or declined?
2. What are the relationships between institutional factors including, size (enrollment), enrollment profile, costs, setting, and control (public or private) and new library building size and cost?
3. What are the leading factors motivating planning for new academic library buildings?
4. What are the leading attributes and characteristics of academic library buildings completed between 2003 and 2009?
5. How are new academic library buildings being used?

Discussing the Study: An Overview

Throughout the discussion of results of the current study, data will be compared with earlier studies to provide frameworks and identify themes among academic library buildings constructed in recent years. For example, in examining building characteristics, the extent to which these characteristics compare and/or continue those of academic library building projects completed between 1995 and 2002 as described by Shill and Tonner (2003) is explored. For factors motivating planning and design of new library buildings, results are compared to conclusions reached by earlier researchers (Bennett, 2003; Freeman, 2005) about the extent to which academic libraries are designed beyond traditional services, print collections, and operational imperatives towards student learning. Library planning is also discussed in the context of built pedagogies (Monahan, 2002) and other frameworks for educational architecture. For new library building characteristics and usage, some results from the current study are compared to earlier observations and research (Shill & Tonner, 2003; Crawford, 1998; Fisher, 2005) to identify similarities, differences, and emerging themes in library use and design. Finally, another important area of inquiry, the relationship between new academic building and physical collections, is explored to gain a general understanding how new libraries incorporate print collections into new buildings and plan for print collections in the coming years. Questions about space planning for physical collections offer new insights on library leaders' views on the relevancy and future of print collections given the ever-increasing amount of information available in digital formats.

This study begins with an overview of literature and research on library history, planning and design, educational architecture theory, and types of projects over the past two decades. An outline of the study's research design follows in chapter 3. The discussion of research design includes an explanation of strategies used for identifying new academic library building projects. This discussion also includes a detailed explanation of the methods used for identifying a range of information on project costs along with important institutional characteristics such as enrollment, size and setting, tuition, Carnegie classifications, etc. Also included in this chapter is a detailed discussion on factors that informed and later framed the design of the survey sent to each library identified as having been completed between 2003 and 2009.

Results of this study are presented in two parts. The first set of results, presented in chapter 4, include a discussion of the scope and pace of academic library construction in recent years. This basic information is coupled with a range of institutional and project data to provide an analysis of where library building is occurring across the landscape of U.S. higher education. This section also uses general descriptive statistical tools to describe size and cost of new library building projects in general as well alongside specific institutional characteristics such as private/public control, institutional size and setting, and enrollment profile, among others. This chapter concludes with a comparison and analysis of new academic library construction between 1996-2002 and 2003-2009.

Results of the survey begin in chapter 6 with a discussion of planning for new library buildings. In this section, responses to a range of questions about pre and post project planning are categorized and summarized. Information about the age of buildings being replaced is included, as are sources of funding for new library projects. A major portion of this chapter is devoted to series of questions that asked respondents to rate the importance of a range of planning factors for their new buildings. This chapter concludes with a discussion, based on current and future book acquisitions data provided by survey respondents, of the changing relationship between planning, design, and use of the library space and physical collections.

It is hoped that this study will provide numerous illustrations of the evolving characteristics of the modern library space. That discussion begins in chapter 7 with an investigation of size of new academic buildings compared with the buildings they augmented or, in most cases, replaced. Technology, both public area and overall infrastructure, is discussed in this section, as is the expansion of general use and soft seating in new libraries. Finally, a detailed analysis of one of the benchmarks of new academic library space, multiuse, is provided using responses to a range of survey questions about use of the library space for non-library purposes, as well as differences in multiuse function between the former space and the new building.

User space has numerous dimensions in new academic libraries. Results from a broad survey section on user space are outlined in chapter 8. Contemporary thinking about academic building design informs the necessity of flexible and varied types of user space for a successful academic library. For academic libraries, user space includes learning space such as collaborative study space, classrooms, traditional quiet study as well as community space and, finally faculty space. Survey participants offered a wealth of information on how user space has been reconceived in new library spaces. These responses also included information on key differences in the types and levels of user space—particularly learning space—between the former library buildings and the new facilities. This chapter concludes with a discussion of survey data that indicate what spaces in these new buildings best represent the library's evolving role in the academic as well as social and cultural life of the institution.

The presentation of survey results concludes in chapter 9 with a discussion of usage of new academic libraries. Pre and post project use of the facilities was reported by most respondents, which provide a baseline (albeit a very basic one) for measuring the success of new library buildings. However, respondents were also asked in this section to provide open-ended responses to questions about specific spaces in these new buildings. Participants were also asked to provide examples of spaces in their new facility that best reflect the library's role in the academic as well as social/cultural life of the institution. All of these data provide rich and colorful evidence of a rapidly evolving academic library space.

Throughout this book, study results are integrated with the discussion of findings. As mentioned, observations from previous studies are included in the conversation, as is, of course, information, data, and commentary from other scholars, researchers, and practitioners across academic librarianship and other disciplines. Readers should be able to use all or selected sections of this research as they require for their purposes. For example, a reader interested in how learning space is incorporated in new library design will find both a presentation of results data as well as a discussion of implications of these data in chapter 8. For those interested specifically in the leading factors that inform new library building planning, study results, discussion, and analysis of planning factors are included in chapter 6. This study concludes with a wrap-up and discussion of what may lie ahead for the academic library building.

chapter two

THINKING ABOUT LIBRARY SPACE

Academic libraries have always been places associated with complexity, authority, and tradition. As the Internet era enters its second decade, however, and the pace of digitization across most disciplines accelerates, academic libraries have been compelled to re-evaluate their purpose and mission. The digital age has not raised so much the question of if academic library buildings will survive but how these facilities will evolve, how successful they will be, and what kind of activities will occur there.

By examining the evolution of the American academic library building, this overview of recent research and writing on academic library space begins by placing the library in its historical context in American higher education, followed by a lengthier exploration of articles and reports on library spaces built over the past decade. General characteristics and attributes of new library spaces within the context of the library's evolving educational mission are also described, as is the library's response to the growth of new modes of student learning. Equally important, the balance of traditional library space with social, collaborative spaces in new library buildings as an emerging design theme in library buildings is outlined through examples of recent building projects as well as theories of educational architecture. This balance is often negotiated in the library building planning process, a subject on which several articles have been published in recent years. Finally, this overview of research also highlights thinking from architects, librarians, and others on the continued importance of new academic library buildings in providing the academic community with a transcendent place and an iconic center for university life.

History

The expansion of the American academic library building over the past two centuries has been, until recently, based on physical collections. In the colonial era, academic library collections consisted of mainly religious texts and foreign language textbooks, and access was restricted. The function of what would now be considered an undergraduate library was assumed by privately supported student literary and debate society libraries, where collections were often much larger and access much less restricted than the college library. By the late antebellum period, however, an early map of the modern higher education system began to form (Atkins, 1991). The emergence of the applied arts, the growth of American publishing, and the onset of curricular reforms that were to continue in the coming decades resulted in the emergence of the academic library as an increasingly important part of the university. Stephen Atkins' 1991 text, *The Academic Library and the American University*, compares enrollment growth with the development of the fist sizable library collections at institutions such as Harvard University, Yale University, and the University of Pennsylvania, which remain among the country's largest academic libraries today.

The rise of science, engineering, and the applied arts; the growth of scholarship and subject specialties and accompanying end of the last vestiges of the recitation mode of learning in higher education; the expansion of the public university system; and the birth of graduate education-oriented research universities (i.e., the University of Chicago; Stanford University) are some of the major factors that gave rise to the modern academic research library (Atkins, 1991). It was in this period that the library became the center of the university. Size and aesthetics mattered greatly, and the number of volumes and grandeur of the library building became, like so many other edifices on campus during the late 19th and early 20th centuries, a matter of prestige. In the post-World War II period, during several decades of growth, the library became the flashpoint for curricular turf battles that continue today. Tension (and influence over library collection budgets) emerged between liberal arts faculty who valued the library as a place of learning (the "heart" of the university) and social science/science/engineering faculty who viewed the library as a center for information exchange (Atkins, 1991).

The debate over the library as access point versus the library as a center for learning has taken on renewed meaning as the educational, cultural, and social role of the library in university life emerge as important design considerations for new academic library buildings (Demas, 2005; Peterson, 2005; Bennett, 2003). Thus, while housing print collections remains an important consideration for new libraries, it has become one of many considerations, and often not the most important consideration. Outcomes of the debate over the function of the academic library space can be found in the forms these buildings have taken in recent years.

Characteristics of New Library Space

The past two decades have been a time of significant transition for the academic building. During the 1990s, colleges and universities invested approximately half a billion dollars a year on library construction projects (Bennett, 2003). Tom Findley, the architect who designed the University of Nevada's state-of-the-art Lied Library, finds no evidence in new library construction to suggest that libraries are getting smaller (Boone, 2002).

Over the past two decades, technology has obviously reshaped library services, collections, and, of course, the library's physical space. The emergence of the Internet as a vehicle for delivering scholarly information has altered the way people use the library and has caused library planners to rethink the library's traditional role in academic life. The relevance of the library physical space has in part endured as a result of the physical library's ongoing transformation. Several themes are beginning to emerge. These themes form a framework for identifying and understanding the changes that are occurring in academic libraries across the country. The transformed library space is often a dual expression of the library's traditional role as a place of books and contemplation along with its emerging role as a place for learning and collaboration. Demas (2005) identifies five core reasons people still come to the library: security, choice, comfort, learning, and serendipity.

Articles, studies, and reports over the last decade have chronicled the changes occurring in the academic library as well as factors informing and influencing these changes. Descriptions of library building and renovation projects address several major themes in modern library design. These include the library as a place for collaboration; learning; high technology; multiuse of new library space; and, of course, long-established functions such as providing a place for print collections. There is wide debate in the library literature as to the scope and efficacy of some factors affecting decisions in new library space design and the level of importance these factors place on the library's traditional mission. At the center of this debate is the consideration of the book and its continued importance in education and research, although most researchers believe that the medium will remain prevalent for the foreseeable future (Demas, 2005; Bazillion & Braun, 2001). This debate has obvious implications for the future of the library space. The emerging importance of information literacy and the library's increasing role in the classroom is changing the way librarians and other educators think about the library space. Another important issue for the academy is the balance between reinventing the library space while retaining the role of the library building as an enduring icon of academic life. As library building projects proceed on campuses across the country, research has begun to focus on assessing the success of these projects through measurements ranging from general library usage patterns to detailed quantitative data. Information on library usage as measured in gate counts and other metrics also exists in publicly available resources such as the Department of Education's National Center for Educational Statistics biennial survey of academic libraries.

Another theme that emerges from reports and descriptions on new and/or redesigned library buildings is the value being placed on incorporating increasingly sophisticated technology and technology-related services into new space. The "information commons" is one of the most widely recognizable expressions of the growing emphasis the academic library is placing on technology in the library space. The information commons is typically a set-aside area, often quite large, that contains computers and peripherals for library patron use. Along with the technology, the information commons is often populated by librarians as well as technology assistants. A variety of library and non-library-related services are offered.

In their extensive inventory of academic library building and renovation projects completed between 1995 and 2002, Shill and Tonner (2003) identify technological infrastructure expansion and the addition of new computing areas as among the most common elements in new libraries. Beagle (1999) claims that the library often faces difficulties when trying to retrofit its traditional, print-based function in the electronic environment and suggests that the information commons, as a service delivery tool, provides a suitable replacement for the longstanding reference desk model. Moreover, technology often requires more rather than less space than traditional library materials and furniture (Boone, 2002). Study seating is also getting larger, with tables and carrels being designed to accommodate a patron's laptops and other digital devices as well as books (Michalak, 1994).

Another characteristic of new library space is multiuse, reversing a trend in previous decades towards "purification" of the academic library building by removing non-library operations (Freeman, 2005). Researchers such as Shill & Tonner (2003) describe the increasing inclusion on non-library facilities in new library buildings. These types of facilities can range from coffee shops to faculty offices. As institutions attempt to maximize square footage on increasingly landlocked campuses, a perception that the library can sacrifice space once needed for bound volumes often infuses the opinions of university planners. Shill and Tonner warn, however, of the consequences of short-sighted thinking in this regard as scholarly publishing specifically and book publishing in general continue to increase. In her outline of three models for the academic library of the future, King (2000) claims that multiuse facilities will become more common as libraries more closely align with the educational goals and overall institutional culture of their organizations.

Many recent library building projects and large-scale renovations have incorporated traditional library features such as quiet study rooms, reading rooms, and an emphasis on physical collections. Library planners make strong arguments for retaining, and in some cases expanding, areas for quiet study and contemplation. Freeman (2005) reports that most students value acoustical privacy in the library and identify reading rooms or similar spaces as their favorite areas of the building. As the library becomes a more collaborative, active place, many libraries are establishing acoustical boundaries once thought unnecessary due to longstanding, implied rules for quiet throughout the library building. Users often sanctify the space by developing a "culture of silence" (Fisher, 2005). Crawford (1998, 1999) outlines the case for a hybrid model in the new academic library space, one that reflects the library's traditional mission (e.g., housing print collections) as well as its evolving mission. For this to be achieved, Crawford argues, the user must be able to experience the library as a place of serious, solitary learning and discovery as well as group learning.

As libraries depart from design constraints of the past decades, an increasing awareness of the building's relationship with the environment is evident in building design and use (Ranssen, 2002; Sannwald, 2001). In general, there is a greater use of glass to link the external and internal space (Harrington, 2001). An emphasis on natural lighting is common in many new academic library buildings. A report on the new library addition to Duke University's Perkins Library describes the popularity of the upper floors of the facility due to natural lighting (Lombardi & Wall, 2005). The relationship to the environment is also reflected in the growing emphasis on sustainable architecture, which has become a major trend in library design (Harrington, 2001) and is prevalent in many recent library building projects, especially those completed within the last five years.

Perhaps the most notable characteristic of new academic library buildings, however, is the inclusion and expansion of space related to the library's role in teaching and learning. As instruction in the use of research materials has expanded to include information in an ever-widening variety of formats, especially digital formats, libraries have expanded information literacy programming and added more classrooms. In addition to classroom and other instructional space, collaborative and communal learning space has emerged as one of the most important design elements in new academic library buildings.

The Library's Role in Learning

Information literacy—the ability to discover and evaluate information in an increasingly complex information environment—is becoming an important element in undergraduate (and often graduate) curricula and educational outcomes. The library's role in teaching information literacy has had an effect on library space planning, especially as it relates to classrooms and flexible learning environments for faculty, student, and librarian interactions. Any discussion of information literacy begins with the library's role in ensuring information quality. Albanese (2003) discusses a "post Internet bounce" in the academic library as faculty and students realize that not all information is available electronically and, even in digital environments, the quality control assured by librarians is indispensable for scholarship and critical thinking (p. 36). Crawford (1999) describes the relationship between emerging library instructional services and newly expanded library spaces.

Dougherty and Adams (2001) outline several key characteristics and limitations of digital information and the challenges presented to student and faculty researchers by these limitations. These challenges include un-reviewed information, commercialized information, complexity, and plagiarism. They argue that the academic librarian occupies an advantaged position to teach users effective strategies for navigating complex information environments—and, in designing new physical library spaces, planners should articulate the role of the library in mediating the access and delivery of high quality information in digital as well as print environments. Then director of libraries at the University of Michigan, William Gosling (2000) argued that the library as a service institution will remain vital as the growth of digital information creates new challenges for researchers in identifying and evaluating scholarly information. Academic librarians are experiencing renewed demand for their expertise due to user dissatisfaction with the lack of authority and control in electronic resources. Furthermore, early expectations of increased user self-sufficiency in navigating electronic resources were overly optimistic; at the University of Michigan, this resulted in the reallocation of staff resources to support information literacy efforts across curricula (Gosling, 2000).

While students value library services that support their learning (Peterson, 2005), some librarians argue that the modern library physical design has not placed enough priority on student learning. Bennett (2005) argues that two major factors are essential for successful learning in the library environment: time on task and domestication of more public spaces on campus. Library spaces need to allow for students to be able to govern the social as well as solitary dimensions of their study environments in order to learn effectively, and libraries should be places that "honor" study and promote an environment for "sustained engagement with academic work" (Demas, 2005, p. 28). The library allows students the pleasure of being alone, and students appreciate the fact that it is socially acceptable to be alone in the library (Demas, 2005). The enduring importance of space that addresses a "deep humanistic urge for personal thought and reflection" (Foote, 2004, p. 44) remains critical to new library design. Quiet space need not be solitary space, of course, and the new library's diverse interior environments must provide for the kind of communal study space that "fosters a silent exchange of energy" as "quiet study is in truth an active experience" (Ranseen, 2002, p. 204). Grand reading rooms are being included in many new academic library spaces and are being restored in existing libraries to accommodate more readers (Foote, 2004).

Several writers and researchers have catalogued space transformations along with new library construction over the past decade. The most common theme in all of the projects described is the importance being placed on including new learning and communal spaces in the library. Albanese's (2006) description of the new academic library at the University of Louisville focuses on the facility's importance as a user- centered space that offers multiple classroom and group study areas. In his outline of questions for library planners devising new facilities, Scott Bennett, Yale University's Librarian Emeritus, stresses the importance of creating spaces that will encourage productive study in a collaborative environment, and for librarians to evaluate the effectiveness of the learning space on an ongoing basis (Bennett, 2005).

McDonald (2002) urges library planners not to forget the importance of including a variety of learning environments in new designs, including areas for quiet, non-collaborative learning. Bennett (2007) identifies several design elements in the new East Commons space in the Georgia Institute of Technology library that include flexible, extendible spaces for group study that were incorporated as a result of principles outlined by the Council on Library and Information Resources. Albanese's (2006) description of the new library at the University of Louisville provides a similar account of state-of-the-art group study spaces. Crawford (1999) offers a list of priorities for the academic library space in the 21st century, encouraging library planners to balance group study as well as other collaborative spaces with the continuing need for space for traditional library activities. The aforementioned Council on Library and Information Resources report describes the increasing popularity of the academic library as a collaborative, social space as a result of new design influences (Freeman, 2005). User groups differ in their expectations of the library as a communal space; students are leading the pace of change in this regard (Weise, 2004).

The character of library study space matters, and more knowledge about new modes of learning (e.g., collaborative learning) should be incorporated into planning for new buildings (Bennett, 2005). Increasingly, pedagogy drives design (Albanese, 2006). The library should be an extension of the classroom, yet much of the academic library design in the 1990s was not systematically informed by new modes of student learning (Bennett, 2003). Bennett's (2003) study of planning motivators for new academic library buildings ended, however, as many new buildings that placed more emphasis on learning spaces were being constructed. Lombardi and Wall (2005) offer an account of the new Bostock Library at Duke University, describing a facility that emphasizes the library's pedagogical function:

> This rediscovery of the library as place is accompanied by a redefinition of the library as facilitator, helping guide the new undergraduate curriculum while ensuring that Duke's students leave the university with a level of information literacy that equips them for a lifetime of learning and leadership in a post digital era. (p. 17.8)

The authors go on to detail an increase in content questions to reference librarians in the new facility accompanied by a decline in directional questions, which is a sign of good building design as well as well as a learning-focused library. Other researchers describe the library's expanding role in the curriculum and its effect on modern library design (Freeman, 2005; King, 2000; Lewis, 2007). Still others outline the library's emerging role as a producer of scholarly information and its influence on space design in general (Lewis, 2007).

Physical Collections and the Library Space

The debate over the future of the book has had an interesting, if not predictable, effect on academic library space planning. Many academic libraries—especially research libraries—have continued to plan for growth in physical collections. While there are many reasons for this, the most prevalent are continued reliance on the monograph as the primary medium for knowledge transmission in many disciplines; growth in annual number of scholarly monographs published; and, perhaps most important, the role of the monograph in developing intellectual capacity.

Dilevko and Gottleib (2002) examined undergraduate use of print journals and monographs and found that over one-third of students prefer print journals to electronic because of a perceived validity of print resources due to the additional information (i.e., diagrams) they provide. The researchers also discovered that undergraduates overwhelmingly prefer books for important contextual information and, in general, associate print books with higher quality research. Use of online resources, especially in the humanities and the social sciences, was associated with getting "things done quickly and easily, not high quality work" (p. 391). Those research findings reinforce the opinions expressed in an Association of College & Research Libraries paper that link the book collection with the interests of classroom faculty (Hardesty, 2000). Dilevko and Gottleib conclude that libraries should consider the marketing power of book collections even as they move towards Internet-centered models.

Use and emphasis on print collections varies according to discipline, and library buildings are accordingly affected depending on library type and function. Different disciplines will migrate literature to digital formats at varying rates, resulting in continuous growth in print collections in many subject areas for several decades to come. Michalak (1994) makes the point that as "long as large numbers of print-based titles are being produced, people will want to read them, and libraries will be expected to house them and make them available" (p. 97). Sannwald (2001) argues that the number of books acquired by "all types of libraries" may not increase dramatically in the coming years but will certainly remain at least at current levels (p. 155). Architects are still designing libraries with print collections in mind, including provisions for robotic storage systems and compact shelving. As library architect Tom Findley pointed out, the printed word is not "disappearing nearly as quickly as some futurists have predicted" (Boone, 2002, p. 390). While print collections are unlikely to disappear any time soon, Hickey's 2001 study of several new academic libraries completed between 1995 and 1999 revealed the majority of these libraries can accommodate print collection growth for only 15 years or less. Hickey also cautions that, as libraries move more print material to compact storage or even offsite, the material will inevitably be used less often, creating a "hierarchy of information" that favors newer material both print and electronic (p. 14).

Crawford (1998, 1999) stresses the importance of maintaining and planning for growth in the library's physical space in order to meet the needs of user populations that desire not only access to technology and digital information, but also a library that functions well as a place, especially for "analog" activities such as reading and collaboration. Crawford outlines the economic and ecological problems posed by the all-digital library, if such a thing could ever exist. Problems with this model include much higher costs and a tremendous amount of wasteful, expensive printing as users grapple with pay-per-view pricing for digital books and other material. Digitization is an excellent solution for enabling access to material that would otherwise not be available, but the printed book continues to offer enormous cost, access, and intellectual advantages over electronic data (Crawford, 1999).

In a position paper for the Association of College and Research Libraries (ACRL), Hardesty (2000) adds to Crawford's argument by advising higher education accrediting agencies to exercise careful judgment when accrediting trans-regional and virtual colleges and universities. Hardesty specifically addresses the question of whether a degree-granting institution needs a physical library (and librarians) for accreditation, and cautions that the lack of a library can diminish the core meaning (and by extension, credibility) of an institution of higher education. Hardesty reminds educators and accrediting agencies that accreditation extends to the entire curricula not just basic, often remedial classes that can be delivered over the Internet with similar results as in a large lecture hall. He outlines the limits of electronic information and stresses the importance of physical collections in an age of still-expanding scholarly book publishing, growth in library consortia, and continued importance of print-based disciplines. Furthermore, he argues, while contents of commercially published electronic databases are often unstable, traditional print collections in an academic library are directly influenced by research interests, subject area expertise, and teaching needs of classroom faculty.

Mann (2001) argues that information from digital sources can lack adequate context and does not require the attention span and concentration to learning and deep thought. Because of this, he argues, the book will remain the library's most vital asset. Mann also challenges the notion, popular in information science, that the existence of information (especially electronic information) assures its use. Finally, Demas (2005) argues that serendipity also remains an indispensable part of the research process:

> Serendipitous discovery is a common and treasured experience in libraries. Building expansion and compact shelving allow colleges to keep as much of their collections as possible on campus, preserving the possibility for serendipity in the stacks. (p. 17.8)

Other reasons for the continued importance of the book include the far-reaching restrictions of copyright; continued growth in book publishing; assurance of quality and control in the library's collection; preservation and archival challenges of digital material; and the critical need of a democracy for a literate populace that is able to connect and contextualize ideas. Thomas (2000) discusses the importance of the book as scholarly medium and stresses the importance of strong print collections coinciding with electronic formats. By adding 3.5 million monographs to its browsing collections, the University of Chicago's 42 million dollar library expansion (Schonwald, 2005) offers an example of an institution's unflinching commitment to the printed book. Indeed, the main web page for University of Chicago academics makes a point of the Chicago's commitment to the book by declaring that, while 'many universities are moving print collections to off-site storage, Chicago is in the midst of expanding its library in the heart of campus" (University of Chicago, 2010).

Lewis (2007) argues, however, that print collections and the space they require will become less important not because of the migration of currently published material to digital formats per se, but because the library will assume a greater curatorial role in developing and maintaining new digital collections built on new knowledge as well as existing (often rare) printed material owned by the library. Fisher (2005) on the other hand, argues that resistance of users to read books online and the expansion of reprint publishing ensure that printed books will have a place in the library for some time.

The Library as Place

At many colleges and universities, the main library is at the heart of the physical campus. The importance of the library as a symbol of institutional values and at the center of the institution's intellectual life has long been reflected in academic library architecture. Translating these values into the modern, highly technological and collaborative library space presents several challenges for library planners. A fair amount of commentary and research offers some insight into how library planners are addressing the iconography of the library edifice. McDonald (2002) and Rizzo (2002) both describe the deep personal connection users make with the library space and the growing recognition of the expanding cultural and social role the library is playing on today's college campus. Demas and Scherer (2002) argue that the physical library should be designed according to tenets of "place making," which involves designing spaces that become more than their physical identities. By creating a sense of place that is transcendent (encouraging imaginative understanding and association) and transportive (uplifting and unique), these spaces steer away from library architecture that treats buildings as containers.

In one of the earlier commentaries in the Internet era on the subject of library as place, Dowler (1996) argues that information technology will infuse and invigorate the traditional library with new energy as users search for context and meaning in complex and confusing online information environments. The library as a place, he believes, will remain important because technological solutions, especially those that seek to create digital information environments that simulate physical ones (i.e., the digital bookshelf) ignore human "perspective." Dowler concludes that one of the paradoxes of the library space is that, although it is most often communal, many of us attach deep personal connections with such spaces (or the idea of them) at an early age. The power of such places is supported by research in the social sciences that explores the relationship between behavior and physical space. In describing the current expansion of the University of Chicago's Regenstein Library, Provost Richard Saller offers a similar view in his statement on the importance of library as the most visible reflection of the university's values (Schonwald, 2005).

The library's role in creating community is one of the most important values reflected in the building's architecture. The library "must serve as the principal building on campus where one can truly experience and benefit from the centrality of the institution's intellectual community" (Freeman, 2005, p. 2). Library design from mid-century through the 1980s was utilitarian: functional but more often than not aesthetically mediocre. The current building trend, however, returns the library building to its iconographic status. Libraries are once again "buildings worth caring about" (Harrington, 2001, p. 14). On college and university campuses, new academic libraries are often used as showpieces that functionally and symbolically integrate the past and the future—and are sources of great institutional pride (Hickey, 2001). During the current and coming transitional decades for academic libraries, architecture and design take on added importance. Michalak (1994) describes the situation this way:

> As the library and university proceed through this prolonged period of transition, there will be a continuing need for the library as a social and intellectual commons, an integrative location which, in its accessible and accommodating environment, provides for the university a continuity between the past and future. (p. 105)

The tangibility and the viability of the library are among the factors that make it such a "robust" social institution (Bazillion & Braun, 2001, p. viii). Students associate the library with membership in the scholarly community. The space provides the unique experience of being both public as well as private, and can also be the center of cultural life on campus (Demas, 2005). Those that come to the library building want to "experience something in the library that cannot be had in an office or home, and that something is the drama of community" (Frischer, 2005, p. 50). Whereas the Internet isolates, the library creates community and adds value to students' lives (Freeman, 2005). Library buildings should be informed by a reawakening of "the fact that libraries are about people—how they learn and how they participate in the life of a learning community" (Demas, 2005, p. 25). New academic libraries are gathering places where people congregate for reasons social as well as academic (Finnerty, 2002; Sannwald, 2001). Language used to describe new academic library buildings generally stresses the role of the new facility in strengthening the campus community through "architecture of interaction" (Boone, 2002, p. 392) and moving away from the model of the library as a "gatekeeper" to that of a "gateway" (Lombardi & Wall, 2006, p. 17.2).

Measuring Use

The strength of these new libraries to retain their impact as traditional symbols of academic life while assuming a myriad of new functions reflects the evolving role of the library space in institutional life. As the functions of the library expand, users come to the space for reasons they have always come, including access to print material, research assistance, quiet study, and learning to use library collections. Yet the library also serves as a new kind of learning space: a social gathering space, a meeting space, and a technological space. These changes in the building's functions present new challenges to those measuring use of the library facility. For the multiuse library, traditional usage metrics of use such as gate counts, head counts, and taking note of books and journals left on tables may not be adequate to assess the impact of the new facility.

Several writers and researchers have begun to explore academic library usage patterns in the Internet era. In one of the most extensive studies to date, Schill & Tonner (2004) tracked usage at more than 90 libraries constructed or significantly remodeled between 1995 and 2002. Eighty percent of these libraries experienced usage increases. Using statistical analysis to determine relationships between specific physical attributes and library usage, the authors determined that most technological improvements (i.e., more data outlets, more public workstations, better technology infrastructure) correlated with increased usage. Other attributes that related to increased usage included quality of the work and learning spaces (rather than quantity, which was often found to have no correlation). Other positive correlations were found between usage and basic elements such as availability of natural lighting and overall ambience, suggesting strong user affinity for the library as place. A surprising lack of correlation was found between usage and library location on campus, the presence of coffeehouses and cybercafés in the library, and the number and types of non-library units in the building.

Other usage studies have focused on specific user groups, with some studies filling gaps in research by examining library use by faculty. In a follow-up study to their 2004 investigation of use of faculty designated study spaces at the University of Oklahoma library (2004), Antell and Engel (2006) discovered that faculty use of printed materials in the library decreases with "scholarly age" (year graduate degree earned), yet younger scholars express strong support for the library as a place conducive and necessary for scholarship. This information suggests that the library space is successfully evolving by remaining relevant to younger faculty members for reasons beyond physical collections.

Other researchers have called for improved metrics in measuring library use, with a particular emphasis on developing tools that quantify use of digital collections and services as extensions of the library's physical space. As librarians plan for the future, they need to clearly differentiate between physical and virtual growth in order to place usage increases (or decreases) in proper context (Martell, 2005). A report by the Digital Library Federation and the Council on Library and Information Resources states that, given the effect of new technologies on libraries, traditional library measures fail to address the "full scope" of how libraries are changing and why (Troll, 2002).

Further blurring the picture is the lack of tools (and agreement) for measuring and interpreting library trends across institutions. Academic libraries should establish clear research agendas linked to strategic goals (Potter, 2004). Potter (2004) outlines the research agenda for assessing the success of the Student Learning Center at the University of Georgia. Potter's testable and measurable assumptions of this agenda include heavy building use; high group study activity; increased faculty and student interaction; more use of the new facility for instructional support without reducing the use of traditional library services for more in-depth research; increased undergraduate use; and a positive effect of the availability of online resources on the autonomy and value of the new facility. Wilson (2003) makes the case for libraries to develop "local" research agendas to add context to data provided by large organizations. New measurement techniques are needed not only for recently added systems and services, but also for traditional performance measurement inputs such as space, collections, and staff, along with output measures such as circulation, reserves, interlibrary loan, instruction, gate counts, and use of electronic resources. By refining and recasting these assessment tools in the context of changing user behavior, new methods of scholarship, and shifting publishing models, a more "complete picture" of the changing library can be developed.

Frameworks for Educational Architecture

Current library design is often informed by educational philosophies and other frameworks for education architecture. Monahan's (2002) "built pedagogy," for example, outlines a theory of building and technology design that moves away from "tacit curricula" to embody pedagogies of "freedom and self-discovery" (¶29). Built pedagogy is only possible through flexibly designed spaces that operate along a continuum between behavioral structure imposed by the building and user autonomy.

Five important elements of built pedagogy are fluidity (flow of individuals as well as natural elements such as light and air); versatility; convertibility (this includes the potential for building the possibility of later redesign into the space); scalability; and modifiability (which invites manipulation and appropriation of the space). Closely related to built pedagogy is the concept of sociability which elevates "collective empowerment" and learning through architecture (Monahan, 2002, ¶46).

Built pedagogy and sociability do not limit the ability of the user to engage in solitary work in the library space. Rather, they give the user a choice of behaviors. Lombardi and Wall (2005) discuss the use of built pedagogy as a framework used at Duke University Libraries that informed the "design of physical space that will influence how people behave in the space, encouraging some activities while constraining others. Bennett (2005) comments on the domestication of library space, calling for buildings that reduce the implication of the authority of the librarian (as the classroom implies the authority of the teacher); promote an environment where knowledge can be shared across the disciplines; and enable students to share ideas in an environment free of political structure and undertone.

Intentionally created spaces are deliberately designed to shape learning in the space; learning-centered architecture encourages the "active construction of knowledge by the learner" (Chism, 2006, p. 2.4). Intentionally created spaces are by their nature flexible spaces. An emerging theme in campus architecture, de-centeredness, views learning as an activity that can take place anywhere on campus, not just classrooms and labs (Chism, 2006). Library information commons and group study space are examples of intentionally created, de-centered spaces. Space will increasingly be defined by more criteria (Foote, 2004) and as such should be flexible and intuitive, both for library collections and other physical space (Harrington, 2001).

Planning

As the library building is defined by more criteria, planning for new libraries becomes necessarily more complex. The debate over planning considerations illustrates the diversity of opinion on the importance (and unimportance) of the library building for new as well as traditional purposes such as book collections. Bennett (2003) studied the planning process in academic library projects between 1992 and 2001 and showed that the strongest motivators for academic library building projects were growth in collections and expansion of non-reference library service units. He does little to hide his disappointment in this fact:

> The knowledge base that guides library planning is thus poorly balanced, tilted heavily towards library operations and away from systematic knowledge of how students learn. Learning needs to outweigh operational needs...we are not asking the right questions. Educational issues need to be front and center. (Bennett, 2005, p. 11)

Bennett's criticism of the planning process in 1990s academic library design decries opportunities missed for "community wide ownership" necessary for building library spaces that focus on learning and teaching rather than only on library operations (Bennett, 2005, p. 5). Freeman (2005) echoes Bennett's sentiments and makes the case for library planning better informed by the institution's educational mission:

> Too much space has already been built in the name of library "needs" without any real understanding of the true value or contribution of expanded or renovated facilities to the

> institution's long term future. The library today must function foremost as an integral and interdependent part of the institution's total educational experience. (p. 6)

Bennett highlights the contradictory nature of book collections in modern libraries: on the one hand books remain an important format, on the other they can threaten the purpose and livelihood of a good library, especially if the planning process is dominated by them. It is interesting to note that Bennett's research also found that few library directors that guided building projects in the 1990s expected shelving space for print collections to be a primary planning issue in coming years. This finding in itself invites follow-up research on library projects completed in the decade following Bennett's study. Shill and Tonner's 2003 study of library projects completed between 1995 and 2002, however, showed that a sizable percentage of libraries will exhaust available shelf space within a decade of project completion. This reflects either a lack of effective planning for print collections or a bellwether of how these libraries view the likelihood of large print collections in the coming years. Foote (2002) notes that space planners are reluctant to plan for print collection growth beyond a decade, especially for print journals.

Another common theme in the literature on library planning is the need to ensure that flexibility is included in the design. Bazillion and Braun (2001) point out that libraries coming online today will be in service for 100 years or more. During that time, technology will evolve, as will pedagogy. Moreover, Bazillion and Braun argue, the coming decades will see an end to the centuries-long dominance of print and its place in the academic library space. Obviously, this view is not shared by everyone in the library community (Mann, 2001; Crawford, 1998, 1999; Demas, 2005). To be sure, information technology has emerged as one of the most important planning considerations in academic libraries (Bazillion & Braun, 2001). As the library function of providing access to information occurs increasingly in the digital space, the building will begin to assume other functions (Bennett, 2003). Still, Freeman (2005) cautions, planners should not overemphasize flexibility at the expense of distinctiveness, which is an important benchmark of any library space. Sannwald (2001) stresses the importance of "atmospherics" in library design: elements ranging from lighting to layout that add a sense of place and uniqueness to the library common.

As academic libraries continue the transition to digital collections and "hybrid" buildings containing a mix of print and digital resources and, more recently, learning spaces, debate has begun about the necessity and number of departmental and branch libraries. University leaders are beginning to seek opportunities to merge specialized libraries into larger "interdisciplinary clusters," ending decades of ownership of branch libraries by departments (Michalak, 1994). The recently completed Lewis Science Library at Princeton University combines the "collections and staff of the Astrophysics, Chemistry, Geosciences, Biology, Mathematics, and Physics branch libraries," and will eventually include Princeton's Psychology library as well (Gaspari-Bridges, 2008, p. 1). Hiller (2004) describes the process of branch library reassessment at the University of Washington Libraries that resulted in several branch library closings and consolidations. Internal research that guided decision-making and planning at the University of Washington included survey data showing that faculty and graduate students visit the library physical space primarily to use collections and, in general, prefer to retrieve information online when possible. As more collections are digitized, faculty and graduate student use of the physical library space will continue to decline. Undergraduates, on the other hand, come to the physical library primarily to use the space and library services. The physical library is fast becoming an undergraduate student space. As faculty and graduate student use of the physical library declines, branch library closings and mergers will continue, with the exception of those libraries that remain dependent on print collections and libraries that provide space for learning and collaborative work (Wilson, 2003).

Conclusion

From the first colonial colleges, the role of the academic library has paralleled the growth of higher education in the United States. Since the first significant expansion of U.S. higher education at the beginning of the industrial revolution and the land grant movement in the 19th Century, followed by the post-WWII baby boom and assignment of much of the nation's scientific research responsibilities to higher education in the 20th century, academic library buildings have been designed primarily around growing physical collections. Over the past two decades, digitization and information technology's effect on the library space has been reflected across a range of library operations and services, including the removal of legacy print journal collections and the transformation of the reference area into the ubiquitous "information commons" found in many libraries today. Ironically, technology often consumes more space than traditional study areas and book collections. Multiuse has also become more common as library buildings are beginning to function across a range of institutional purposes. One over-reaching characteristic in new academic library buildings across different types of institutions is the emphasis placed on dedicated space for study, particularly collaborative study. In addition, many traditional elements, namely the availability of quiet space and, often, the iconography of book collections in academic library buildings remain as important today as they have been for generations. Similarly, while growth of physical collections will remain an important though not necessarily primary consideration in library planning, construction of new library spaces such as branch, departmental, and subject libraries for disciplines whose literature has moved rapidly away from printed formats will likely continue to decline as physical collections are consolidated or moved offsite. Library space planning is increasingly informed by changing user expectations and the library's evolving and expanding role in student learning. Several frameworks for educational architecture focus on flexible, intentional, and de-centered educational space and offer applicability for user-centered library design. Most new library buildings experience significant increases in use in the years following opening. As library buildings change, new methods for measuring their use should be devised. Finally, while the book's primacy has lessened in library space design, recent building projects provide growing evidence of the strengthened role of the library building as center of campus life, learning, and a powerful symbol of the institution's scholarly mission.

chapter three

STRATEGIES FOR RESEARCH

Creating an Inventory of New Library Buildings

In order to gain a comprehensive view of academic library construction over the past seven years, it is important to account for the entirety of new libraries built in this period. Therefore, in the research design, it was decided that an inventory of all academic library buildings completed between 2003 and 2008 and later, through 2009 would be created and that all libraries in the inventory would be included in the study. By focusing on new library buildings only, this study differs from earlier studies in that it does not include renovations. Renovations, of course, are an important measure of the level of the investment college and universities make in library space. However, the size and scope of renovations varies widely; moreover, renovations can be constrained by limitations posed by the existing structure. New library buildings offer a clear view of library design without influencing factors associated with retrofitting existing and outdated library space.

Previous studies indicate that information on new library building projects is discoverable and that, in general, the number of buildings completed annually is measurable (Shill & Tonner, 2003). By focusing on new library construction only, adequate time was allowed to target research on discovering these types of projects through a wide range of data sources. This work proved valuable in filling gaps and verifying and revising data collected from respondents to the survey that was sent to each new library in the study, which will be discussed in the next chapter. The number of libraries for inclusion in this study was further refined by limiting the subset to new buildings constructed at four-year and above, not-for-profit institutions. In addition, as many new buildings in the study were expected to be additions to existing structures, only additions that closely approximated or exceeded the size of the original structure were considered for inclusion in this study.

Information on new academic library building projects can be found in a variety of sources. As there is no single point of information on these projects, creating an inventory of new library buildings required consulting resources ranging from professional literature to informal networks of library planners, administrators, and architects. Initial work on identifying new library projects began in spring 2008. At that time, several sources of information were identified through previous studies and literature searches as well as first-hand knowledge. Researchers and practitioners in library space planning were also consulted. By fall 2008, 85 academic library construction projects completed between 2003 and 2008 were identified as meeting the criteria for inclusion in the study. Libraries completed in 2009 were added to the inventory in early 2010. Two major sources in the professional literature for information on library building projects are the annual architecture issues of *American Libraries* (published in April) and *Library Journal* (published in December). These issues list information on new library projects across the country, including project types (e.g., renovations and additions versus new construction), square footage, architects, and project costs. These resources were reviewed back to 2003 and various information on new building projects (e.g., size, year completed, costs) were cross-checked against institutional websites and other sources for listed institutions. These resources were also consulted in building a list of library projects completed between 1996 and 2002, the seven year period immediately preceding the current study. In December 2008 and again in December 2009, the annual architectural issues of *Library Journal* were checked to ensure all of the new 2007–2008 and 2008-2009 academic library projects listed there were included in the study. Library projects identified in *Library Journal* are also listed in the *Bowker Annual of Library and Book Trade Information*, which was also used to cross-check information.

Another important resource for information on academic library construction is *The Chronicle of Higher Education's* Campus Architecture section, which contains news and information on a range of academic building projects across the U.S., including libraries. *The Chronicle*'s online database of academic building projects begins in 2003 and contains numerous library construction and renovation projects. In addition, *The Chronicle*'s criterion for building additions versus renovations was used as a guide for including libraries in this study. This criterion is partially derived from definitions of new construction used in *The Chronicle of Higher Education*'s Campus Architecture database (*The Chronicle of Higher Education*, 2008).

Information on academic law and medical library building projects is maintained by the American Bar Association (ABA) and the American Association of Health Sciences Libraries (AAHSL). AAHSL compiles a list of medical library building projects on the organization's website. A small number of academic medical library projects completed since 2003 were identified using this resource. The ABA maintains a resource guide for law school facilities that includes data on law library projects over the past several years. The ABA recommends that law library planners use Schooldesigns.com, which maintains a partial list and project descriptions of library facilities constructed since 2000. This resource was used to identify several new libraries for the study population as well as verify and add to information for projects identified using other sources.

The Library Leadership and Management Association (LLAMA), a section of the American Library Association (ALA), provides information on academic library building projects through its Building and Equipment Section (BES). Through its discussion groups and sponsored programs at LLAMA institutes and ALA meetings, BES also provides excellent communications channels for learning about library construction projects, trends in library design, and cost and management issues associated with new library buildings. The study was discussed at LLAMA BES discussion group meetings at the 2008 and 2009 ALA annual meetings, as well as the 2010 ALA Midwinter meeting. The 2008 ALA annual conference in Anaheim, California, featured several presentations by leading library architects and planners, as well as a biannual building design awards presentation co-sponsored by the International Interior Design Association (IIDA) and LLAMA. Most of these meetings included project descriptions of new academic library buildings, renovations, and additions from a variety of perspectives. Information from these sessions yielded data on a small number of recently completed library building projects not previously identified for this study. Follow up phones calls and emails were made to several architects in order to identify library building projects not discussed at the ALA conference. In July 2008, and in January 2010, emails were sent to the LLAMA/BES email distribution list seeking information on new library projects that may have been missed. Responses to these messages were used to identify a small number of new projects for the study population as well as gain more information on previously discovered projects. In addition to the LLAMA/BES email distribution list, notification of the study was also sent to the Academic Library Advancement and Development Network (ALADN) email distribution list. Responses from this group also yielded information in a small number of previously unidentified projects.

As there is no single source for information on new academic library construction, developing such a resource remains an excellent opportunity for any one of the various professional organizations (or individuals) that collect information on academic library building projects. Moreover, there are often inconsistent data on project characteristics depending on which source one consults. Creating an inventory of library projects for this study involved making determinations as to what sources were more current and most authoritative. In general, data such as fact sheets and press releases published by the institutions themselves were considered authoritative. Given the broad array of resources necessary to consult, there may have been some projects that were missed. However, given the extensiveness of the search and selection process, it is believed that the current inventory includes most of the new academic libraries completed at four-year institutions in the United States between 2003 and 2009.

Institutional Data for Colleges and Universities that Built New Libraries

Data about the institutions that built new academic libraries between 2003 and 2009 were derived from a variety of resources. This information was used to build a framework for analyzing trends in library building in U.S. higher education during the study period. Institutional data were obtained from the Carn-

TABLE 1
Variables Used to Describe Libraries in the Study

Variable	Description	Data Source(s)
Year	Initial year new facility completed	Various
State	State or U.S. Territory	Various
Library	Library name	Various
Institution	College or university	Various
Carnegie Classification	Baccalaureate, master's colleges, doctoral/ research, or special focus (specialty) institution	Carnegie Foundation for the Advancement of Teaching (Carnegie)
Public/Private	Governance/control	Carnegie
Residential/Non-residential	Campus setting	Carnegie
Total Enrollment	Total FTE and PTE	IPEDs
Enrollment Profile*	Dominant student enrollment at undergraduate/ graduate levels	Carnegie
Cost of Attendance	Annual tuition and fees	IPEDs
Library Project Cost	Total project cost	Various
Library Project Cost Per Student	Project cost/FTE and PTE enrollment	Derived from other variables
Cost Per Square Foot	Total Project Cost/Total Square Footage	Derived from other variables
Library Square Footage	Library size	Various

egie Foundation for the Advancement of Teaching via the foundation's online database at www.carnegiefoundation.org and the Integrated Postsecondary Education Data System (IPEDs) at nces.ed.gov/ipeds/. Library building project data that could not be derived from the library literature were obtained from sources including institutional press releases, library websites, and news articles. Data were then organized into variables that complete the framework. Some variables were taken directly from data sources while others were revised for the purpose of organizing the libraries within distinct categories. Table 1 lists the variables used to describe the 99 libraries included in this study and the sources used to obtain data used in defining the variable.

All data used to derive these variables were obtained from publicly available sources. The variable "Carnegie classification" organizes institutions in four categories that describe institutional enrollment and curricular focus in general terms. In describing institutions, a slightly revised scheme for Carnegie classifications was devised for this study: doctoral granting universities are not differentiated by level of research activity as defined by the 2005 revision of Carnegie classifications ("Very High Research" and "High Research") and include all universities that grant at least 20 doctoral degrees per year (Carnegie Foundation, n.d.). Master's institutions include all three levels of master's degree-producing institutions in the 2005 revised Carnegie classifications. Baccalaureate colleges include all exclusively undergraduate institutions but also, as the "threshold level of master's degree production separating Baccalaureate and Master's institutions" has changed with the Carnegie classification revisions, some institutions that previously "would have been classified among Master's Colleges" (Carnegie Foundation, n.d., Basic Classification Description, ¶13).

Carnegie "size and setting" classifications describe campuses according to different levels of resident versus non-resident student populations. "Highly" and "primarily" residential colleges/universities have more than half and between 24% and 49% of students living on campus, respectively. Highly and primarily nonresidential institutions have more than half and between 24% and 49% of students living off campus, respectively. For the purposes of this study, the former group is assigned the variable "residential," the latter group "non-residential."

Information on the institution's enrollment profile was identified to determine how undergraduate and graduate enrollment levels distributed among the institutions that built new libraries. Carnegie defines "very high undergraduate" and "high undergraduate" institutions as institutions having less than 10% and between 10% and 24% graduate and/or professional student enrollment, respectively. Carnegie defines "majority undergraduate" institutions as having between 24% and 49% graduate/professional student enrollment. Many large colleges and comprehensive universities fit into the high undergraduate and majority undergraduate enrollment profiles. Carnegie defines majority graduate/professional institutions as having more than half full-time equivalent enrolled in graduate programs. The variable "cost of attendance" includes undergraduate tuition and fees for academic year in which the library was completed, up to library's completed in 2008 and 2009. At the time the results of this study were being prepared, tuition data beyond 2007 were not yet available via IPEDS. While this may present a slight imbalance between library project costs for buildings completed in 2008-2009 with current tuition levels, it is believed that the difference does not significantly affect general findings of any possible relationship between cost of attendance and what institutions spend on new library buildings. Finally, for public institutions, in-state tuition and fees are used and, for institutions with majority or exclusively graduate student populations, graduate program tuition was used.

Survey Design

By building on earlier studies (Bennett, 2003; Shill & Tonner, 2003), the survey portion of this study addressed a research problem using a study that "replicates a past study but examines different participants and different research sites" (Creswell, 2008, p. 72). Although some inferential data were gained, the main focus of the survey was to explore the qualities of a population rather than "relating variables or predicting outcomes" (Creswell, 2008, p. 388). The value of this research was increased by introducing an entirely new, unstudied group: new academic library buildings completed between 2003 and 2009. One of this survey's main purposes was to explore the characteristics of new academic library buildings and compare those findings to data from studies conducted in earlier timeframes (primarily the 1990s). This study sought to identify building trends, and in doing so adds to the current body of knowledge about academic library buildings in the digital age. This study also sought to identify specific factors related to the planning of the academic library building.

In April, 2008, a pilot study was conducted in order to finalize design of the survey instrument; to evaluate the survey for technical functionality and usability; and, most importantly, to test the survey with a small number of library deans and directors. The scope, content, and design of the survey were also discussed with authors of previous studies. These activities resulted in a significantly streamlined and focused survey instrument.

As previously stated, unlike previous studies, this study did not include renovations. Building additions were included only if they approximated or exceed the size of the original structure. The study was also limited to four-year, not-for-profit institutions, beginning with baccalaureate and extending through master's, doctoral, and special focus institutions as defined by classifications used by the Carnegie Foundation for the Advancement of Teaching. The subset was identified through extensive searching of professional literature, annual guides/serials, databases, and results from inquiries to library architects, planners, and practitioners. In the first phase of the study, the subset was analyzed for approximation to the overall population of four-year institutions in the United States and its territories.

This survey instrument (see Appendix A) included close-ended questions to ascertain planning factors for building new facilities, specific building attributes and characteristics, and usage data. For building characteristics as well as information on how patrons are using the new library space, semi-closed questions were used to explore response possibilities. Open-ended as well as semi-closed questions were also used to allow respondents to describe in their own words how the new building is being used as well as how specific features and space in the new building reflect the library's academic role as well as the cultural life of the institution. Additional open-ended and semi-closed questions allowed respondents to list factors affecting planning for library collections as well as additional opportunities to provide information on usage metrics, non-library facilities in the new space, and funding sources.

Some of the questions in the survey were adapted from instruments used in earlier studies. These instruments have proven to be reliable and valid, with results of these surveys being presented in two major research articles published within the last decade. (Bennett, 2003; Shill & Tonner, 2003). To expedite response time by not burdening respondents with institutional and building project questions for which reliable data can be found elsewhere, each survey was post-populated with data derived from sources that include the Carnegie Foundation for the Advancement of Teaching and the National Center for Education Statistics. Building project data on library size and cost were provided by respondents but augmented (and, when necessary, verified) with information from databases, project documents and announcements—especially those from the institutions themselves—and the professional literature.

The type of data collected from the survey differs from that collected in the first phase of the study in that the first phase identified several general institutional and project variables for the libraries that were built. The purpose of the survey of the libraries was to gain a deeper understanding of the factors involved in planning new academic libraries, the characteristics and qualities of the facilities, usage, and incorporation of traditional library collections and services in the design of these buildings. The three primary research questions concerning planning, space, and usage were addressed through a range of themes, including the library as a learning space, library collections, and functional differences between the old and new library. In addition to quantitative data, respondents were given the opportunity to provide written responses to a number of questions, adding to the depth of data across several areas of the survey.

Survey design was completed in June 2008. The subset of the population was finalized by August 2008. An email invitation for a web-based survey was sent to library deans and directors on August 25, 2008 and, after the decision was made to extend the study to libraries completed in 2009, on January 3, 2010. This message was personalized to address library directors by surname as well as to identify the specific new building project at his or her institution. The message then described the purpose and significance of the study, invited participation, provided a link to the web survey, and assured confidentiality. Both survey periods ran for approximately 5 weeks, with reminders sent at regular intervals only to those institutions that had not yet responded. The majority of responses came back in the first week of the survey. However, two libraries were completed during or after the survey period had ended. A small number of libraries were eliminated from the study based on project information revealed by the survey respondents that indicated the libraries did not meet the criteria for inclusion in the study, mainly due to completion earlier than 2003. In addition, during the work of extending the study through buildings completed in 2009, two additional libraries completed in late 2008 were identified and added to the inventory. In total there were 58 completed responses to the survey, representing an overall response rate of 59%. Survey results will be discussed in chapters five through nine.

Conclusion

Research design for this study involved several steps. The first step consisted of deciding and then deriving the basic project and institutional variables that would serve as a framework for describing academic library construction activity over the past several years. It was important not only that building projects were described, but also that these primarily quantitative descriptions were linked with institutional information in order to provide data on what kinds of colleges and universities are building new libraries and at what size and cost. Secondly, an inventory of academic library building projects completed between 2003 and 2009 was created using a variety of research tools and strategies. An inventory of new academic library buildings completed between 1996 and 2002 was also created for comparison to the current period. Finally, an extensive survey consisting of questions on new building planning, characteristics, and use was designed and vetted through a pilot study, then sent electronically to library directors at each of the 99 new libraries completed between 2003 and 2009. Data from the survey was later transferred to Microsoft Excel and then imported into SPSS (v.16) for statistical analysis. The next chapter will outline results from the first phase of this study and provide a comprehensive overview of recent academic library construction in the United States.

chapter four

THE BIG PICTURE: AN OVERVIEW OF RECENT U.S. ACADEMIC LIBRARY CONSTRUCTION

New Academic Library Buildings, 2003–2009

There were 99 new academic library buildings completed at four-year, not-for-profit colleges, universities, and special focus institutions across the U.S. and its territories between 2003 and 2009. The year 2004 saw the most new library buildings completed (n=18), and 2006 and 2009 the least, with only 12 new buildings completed in each of those years. Within the study period, new library construction has trended downward since 2003, and significantly downward when compared to the seven year period prior to the current study, which will be discussed later in this chapter. There were an average of 14 new libraries built annually between 2003 and 2009. Figure 1 shows the number of libraries completed by year.

FIGURE 1
New Academic Library Buildings Completed, 2003–2009

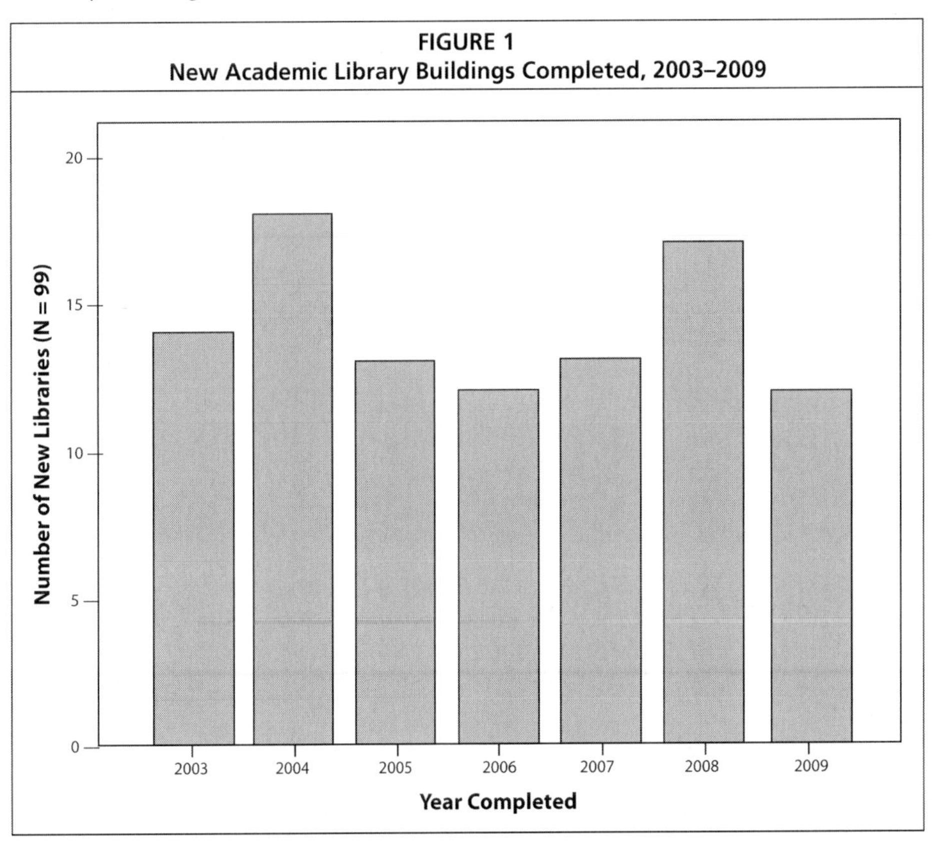

Types of Institutions that Built New Libraries

When compared to the overall population of U.S. not-for-profit four-year institutions, the number of colleges and universities in this study generally approximated the overall population. Doctoral/research universities, however, were represented at higher percentages in the study than in the general population, with values for this category of institutions more than 50% higher than the percentage of doctoral/research institutions in the overall population of U.S higher education. Because of great variability (institutions range from religious schools to technical colleges) and subsequent large number of special focus institutions in the overall population, the six institutions in this

TABLE 2 Approximation of Institutions in Study (N = 94) to General Population by Carnegie Classification				
Type of Institution (Carnegie Class)	Number of Institutions that Built New Libraries (n=81)	Percent of Institutions that Built New Libraries	Number of Institutions in Population	Percent of Institutions in Population
Baccalaureate College	28	30%	693	44%
Master's College/University	33	36%	619	39%
Doctoral/Research Universities	32	34%	275	17%
Total	93	100%	1587	100%

TABLE 3 Approximation of Institutions in Study (N = 99) to General Population by Enrollment Profile				
Enrollment Profile	Number of Institutions that Built New Libraries (n=99)	Percent of Institutions that Built New Libraries	Number of Institutions in Population	Percent of Institutions in Population
Exclusive Undergraduate	16	16%	553	24%
Very High Undergraduate	27	27%	563	25%
High Undergraduate	32	32%	485	21%
Majority Undergraduate	16	16%	257	11%
Majority Graduate/Professional	4	5%	145	6%
Exclusive Graduate/Professional	4	4%	264	12%
Total	99	100%	2267	100%

study categorized as special focus institutions were not included in this analysis of approximation, but are otherwise included in other aspects of analysis. Despite overrepresentation of doctoral/research universities in the study, when one takes enrollment profile into account, institutions that built new libraries approximates somewhat more evenly to the overall population of U.S. colleges and universities, as illustrated in Table 3. Here, only institutions with more than 50% graduate student enrollment deviated markedly from the expected value based on the population.

In order to gain a general understanding of the types of institutions that have built new libraries over the past six years as well as establish a starting point for a more detailed analysis, institutions that built new libraries were cross-tabulated by a number of institutional variables. As in previous studies (Shill & Tonner, 2003), public institutions were represented in greater proportion in the study than in the overall population. Public institutions represent approximately 29% of the overall population of four-year institutions, yet comprise 50% of the institutions that built new libraries between 2003 and 2009. As it was in the Shill and Tonner study, this fact is most likely attributable to far greater enrollments at public universities. The number of public institutions that built new libraries in the study period was approximately the same for public and private institutions (50 publics versus 49 privates). Public, doctoral/research institutions built the greatest number of new libraries

TABLE 4 Institutions Completing New Library Buildings, 2003–2009 by Carnegie Classification and Institutional Control				
		Public	Private	Total
Baccalaureate		10	19	28
	% of Total	10%	19%	28%
Master's		16	17	33
	% of Total	16%	17%	33%
Doctoral/Research		24	8	32
	% of Total	24%*	8%	32%
Special Focus		0	6	6
	% of Total	.0%	6%†	6%
Total		50	49	99
	% of Total	51%	49%	100.0%
*Expected value is 7%; †Expected value is 27%				

between 2003 and 2009, outpacing private, doctoral/research institutions by three to one. While the number of new libraries at master's colleges and universities was roughly equal between private and public institutions, the number of new libraries built at private baccalaureate institutions was nearly double that of public baccalaureate colleges. Not surprisingly, as most special focus institutions are privately controlled, all six of the new libraries built at these schools fit into this governance category.

Expected values of institutions building new libraries based on the overall population (n=2,226) of U.S. not-for-profit baccalaureate, master's, doctoral, and special focus institutions deviated substantially from expected values in two groups: public doctoral and private special focus institutions. In both groups, the percentage values of institutions in the study and institutions in the population differed by more than 50%. Public doctoral institutions represent 7% of the U.S. higher education institutions but comprise 24% of the institutions in the study. Not-for-profit, private special focus institutions represent 27% of the not-for-profit institutions in U.S. higher education but only comprise 6% of the institutions building new libraries (see Table 4).

Enrollment profile provides a more detailed picture, with large percentages of new library construction occurring at institutions with undergraduate populations of more than 90%. Approximately 43% of all new academic libraries built between 2003 and 2009 were at institutions with undergraduate enrollments exceeding 90%, compared to only 22% of the libraries built between 1996 and 2002. While these data indicate an upward trend in library construction at undergraduate institutions in the current period, the expected value for not-for-profit, four-year institutions with greater than 90% undergraduate enrollment is 49% based on the entire population of U.S. not-for-profit four-year institutions. Thus, overall, new library construction at undergraduate institutions over the past seven years is still higher but closer to an approximate balance with the percentage of undergraduate institutions in the overall population. Public institutions with 100% undergraduate, high

TABLE 5 **Institutions Completing New Library Buildings, 2003–2009 (N = 99) by Enrollment Profile and Institutional Control**								
		Enrollment Profile						
		EXU	VHU	HU	MU	MGP	EXGP	Total
Public		8	15	24	6	0	0	50
	% of Total	8%*	15%	24%‡	6§	.0%	.0%	51%
Private		8	12	8	10	4	3	49
	% of Total	8%†	12%	8%	10%	4%	4%**	49%
Total		16	27	32	16	4	4	99
	% of Total	16%	27%	32%	14%	4%	4%	100%

EXU=Exclusively Undergraduate; VHU=Very High Undergraduate; HU=High Undergraduate; MU=Majority Undergraduate; MGP=Majority Graduate; EXGP=Exclusively Graduate/Professional

*Expected value is 4%; †Expected value is 20%; ‡Expected value is 11%; §Expected value is 2%; **Expected value is 11%

undergraduate (more than 75%), and majority undergraduate (more than 50%) enrollments, however, exceeded expected values by wide margins, as seen in Table 5.

Another framework for analyzing academic library construction over the past seven years is campus setting: residential or non-residential. Nearly all of the private universities completing libraries in the study period were residential institutions. Public and private residential institutions did not deviate far from expected values based on the overall population. Public and private non-residential institutions did, however (see Table 6). Between 2003 and 2009, 60% of new library construction occurred on residential campuses, which closely approximated the expected value for residential campuses in the overall U.S. higher education population, as shown in Table 6. Public non-

TABLE 6 **Institutions Completing New Library Buildings, 2003–2009, by Setting and Institutional Control**				
		Residential or Non-Residential		
		Residential	Non-Residential	Total
Public		18	32	50
	% of Total	19%	34%*	54%
Private		41	2	43
	% of Total	44%	2%†	46%
Total		59	34	93
	% of Total	63%	37%	100%

*Expected value is 19%; †Expected value is 14%

residential institutions represented 32% of institutions building new libraries, while these institutions make up only 19% of the overall, four-year, not-for-profit higher education population excluding special focus institutions. Private non-residential institutions were underrepresented, however, with only 2% of private non-residential institutions building new academic libraries even though these institutions comprise 14% of the overall population excluding special focus institutions. Carnegie does not ascribe size and setting classifications to special focus institutions, so those six institutions in the study were not included in this part of the analysis, as reflected in Table 6.

Size and Cost of New Libraries

While linking basic institutional variables with new library projects provides a general overview of academic library construction over the past seven years, a targeted approach to linking specific library project variables with institutional data provides a deeper analysis of patterns across the population. This study took two major indicators of investment in the new library building, size (total square footage) and cost (total building project cost), and measured these against major institutional variables such as enrollment, tuition, size and setting, and control. Foote (2005) claims that, in general, libraries are getting larger. While new library size in relation to the building replaced will be discussed later, general characteristics of the study population suggest that some very large academic libraries have been built in recent years.

Library Size

Between 2003 and 2009, 9,345,853 square feet of new academic library space was constructed, with a mean of approximately 94,400 square feet. Due to the variety of institution and library types as well as the fact that some of the library projects in the study are additions, there is a good deal of variance around the mean. The smallest library is a 4,815 departmental library at a small, private university. The largest library building is a 475,000-square-foot public/academic mixed-use space at a large public university. Public universities built significantly larger library buildings, exceeding the average square footage of libraries at private institutions by a factor of two, as shown in Table 7. Libraries at public colleges and universities are more than three times larger on average than private universities and are built at a lower cost per student. New libraries at non-residential institutions, most of which are public, are also larger. However, while higher square footage for libraries at public institutions is logical in terms of higher enrollments, it does not necessarily translate into more library space, as indicated by square feet per student. An independent samples t-test comparing the means of library square feet per student at public versus private institutions to be significant at the .01 level.

Another variable thought to have an important relationship with library size is institutional setting. One of the hypotheses

TABLE 7
Library Square Footage, Public/Private Institutions

	Library Square Footage		
	N	Mean	Std. Deviation
Public	50	127,376	94,889
Private	49	60,757	44,833

TABLE 8
Library Square Footage per Student, Public/Private Institutions

	Library Square Footage		
	N	Mean	Std. Deviation
Public	50	16	21
Private	49	50	128

TABLE 9 Library Size, Residential and Non-Residential Campuses			
	Library Square Footage, Residential and Non-Residential Setting		
	N	Mean	Std. Deviation
Residential	59	79,824	56,542
Non-Residential	40	115,907	105,131

TABLE 10 Library Square Footage per Student, Residential and Non-Residential Campuses			
	Library Square Footage		
	N	Mean	Std. Deviation
Residential	59	26	35
Non-Residential	40	43	140

of this study was that libraries at residential institutions would be larger as well as more expensive. However, the opposite is true. The average size for new libraries on residential campuses is approximately 80,000 square feet. At non-residential institutions, the average size for new library buildings is significantly higher: approximately 116,000 square feet. In addition to governance and institutional setting, several other institutional and project factors were tested for correlation with library size, as shown in Table 11.

One of the more interesting and significant correlations is the negative correlation between tuition and library size. This correlation remains roughly the same even when removing the one institution in the population that charges no tuition. The correlation indicates that some of the largest and most expensive academic libraries were built at public institutions. Given that the mean tuition at private universities in this study is approximately $23,072 compared to a mean of $4,919 at public universities, it can be assumed that the libraries scattered on the left side of the diagram in Figure 2 are at public institutions. Also, while the correlation between library size and enrollment is significant, one would expect that the value for the correlation would be higher than .221. This discrepancy may be the result of the wide variance of library types in this study (e.g., small departmental and professional libraries at schools with large enrollments) or any number of other factors. Finally, the slightly negative correlation between library size and cost per student and cost per square foot indicates that, to a certain degree, new library building project costs achieve economies of scale as libraries get larger.

The remaining question is how these variables combine to explain library size in terms of library square footage per student. In order to arrive at these data, a model was developed that included continuous institutional and project variables that showed significant correlation with library square footage as well as categorical variables to test for correlation with the

TABLE 11 Correlations with Library Size (Total Square Footage)							
		Square Footage (Size)	Cost per Student	Cost	Cost per Square Foot	Total Tuition	Total Enrollment
Square Footage (Size)	Pearson Correlation	1	–.018	.793*	–.111	–.322*	.221†
	Sig. (2-tailed)		.859	.000	.276	.001	.028
	N	99	98	98	98	97	99
*Correlation is significant at the 0.01 level (2- tailed); †Correlation is significant at the 0.05 level (2-tailed)							

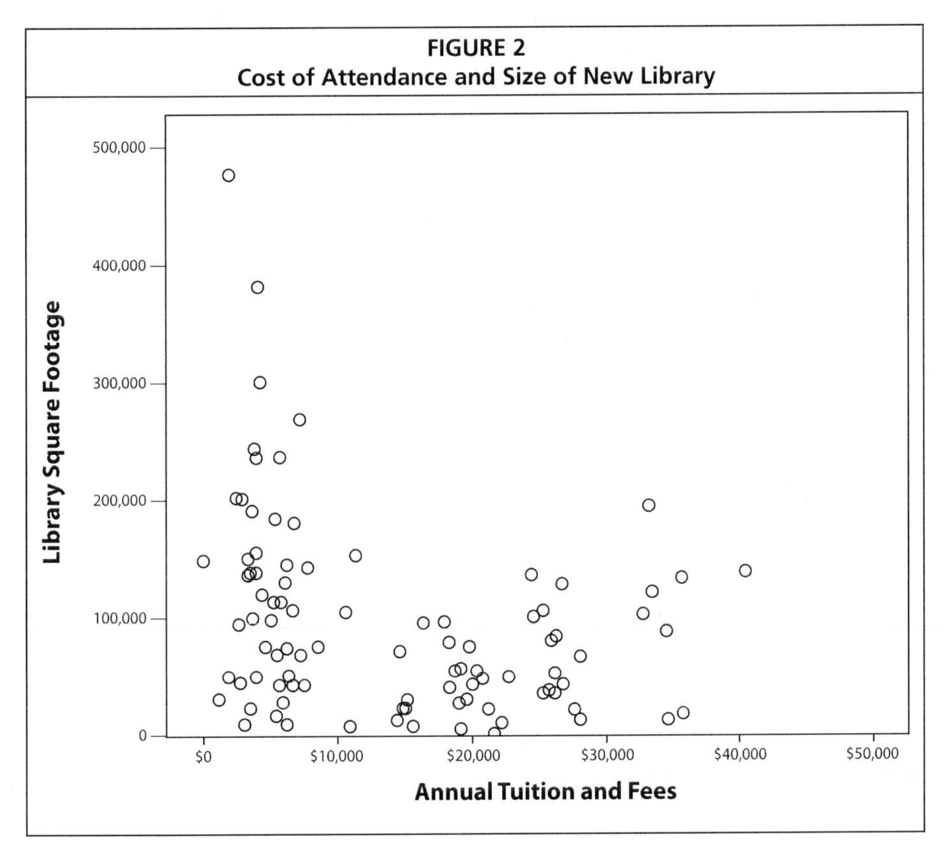

FIGURE 2
Cost of Attendance and Size of New Library

more specific metric, square feet per student. The correlating beta weight should reflect the relationship between the predictor variables and square feet per student while accounting for the range of other variables in the model. Continuous variables ranged from enrollment to cost metrics, while categorical variables included enrollment profile and Carnegie classification. Because of the differences in square footage means between libraries at public and private and residential and non-residential campuses, these variables were also included in the model, which was tested using a statistical regression, and accounts for 36% of the variance in library square footage per student. In this model, the leading predictor of square footage per student is enrollment, which is negatively correlated with the amount of square feet per student in the new building. The greater the number of students enrolled at the institution, the less space per student in the new library. The second leading predictor of library size is public or private control of the institution. Public institutions that completed new libraries between 2003 and 2009 built typically larger libraries but also have larger enrollments. Private institutions with lower enrollments are more likely to offer more library space per student.

While this study of new academic library buildings did not include measures of quality, library square footage per student may be considered such a quality measurement for the sake of this discussion. While a handful of the buildings in the population were smaller specialty libraries at both public and private institutions, most of these new facilities serve as main libraries on their campuses. Using square footage per student as a quality measurement, it appears that private universities have significant advantages over public institutions: library square footage is approximately 50 square feet per student at private institutions but only 16 square feet per student at public institutions. Given the focus on supporting learning-related activities in new academic libraries and the addition of more study space of all kinds in these new buildings, students that have access to more library space may enjoy higher quality learning environments than students with less

TABLE 12 Cost of New Academic Library Buildings, 2003–2009						
	N	Minimum	Maximum	Sum	Mean	Std. Deviation
Cost	98	$1,020,780	$177,500,000	$2,438,325,513	$24,880,873	$25,529,325
Cost per Square Foot	98	$74.04	$1,318.92	$27,405	$280	$168
Cost per Student	98	$38	$82,352	$683.782	$6,977	$10,967

room. There are no doubt various reasons for the discrepancies in the amount of library square feet per student at public versus private institutions, including the fact that public institutions, especially those at large doctoral and research institutions, have several branch and departmental libraries on campus to serve graduate students in various disciplines. Still, given the gap in square footage and the fact that most of the libraries in the study are, again, main libraries for the campus, it is more likely that these differences can be accounted for by higher user expectations at private institutions given the cost of attending and, of course, the financial resources of the institution.

Library space per student also differed markedly depending on whether an institution was residential or non-residential. New libraries at residential institutions offered more than 60% more square feet per enrolled student than new libraries at non-residential institutions. Public, non-residential institutions in the study exceeded expected values based on the overall population, while private, non-residential institutions were under-represented significantly. Public, non-residential institutions, therefore, were far more likely to build new libraries than private, non-residential institutions, but with less library square footage per student.

Library Cost

One of the most important measures of an institution's level of investment is, of course, the cost of the new facility. Approximately $2.4 billion was spent on new library construction between 2003 and 2009. The most expensive building project was $177,500,000, and the least costly was $1,020,780. Cost per student ranged from $38 to a staggering $82,352. On average, colleges and universities in this study spent $6,977 per student on new library facilities, with the variance in institutional types

TABLE 13 Cost of New Library Buildings 2003–2009, Public and Private Institutions				
		N	Mean	Std. Deviation
Cost	Public	50	$30,170,237	$29,188,596
	Private	48	$19,371,118	$19,902,233
Cost per Square Foot	Public	50	$248	$122
	Private	48	$313	$201
Cost per Student	Public	50	$3,554	$5,302
	Private	48	$10,544	$13,909

TABLE 14 Cost of New Library Buildings 2003–2009, Residential and Non-Residential Campuses				
		N	Mean	Std. Deviation
Cost	Residential	58	$23,633,232	$20,146,875
	Non-Residential	40	$27,690,952	$31,970,382
Cost per Square Foot	Residential	58	$309	$195
	Non-Residential	40	$237	$105
Cost per Student	Residential	58	$7,015	$7,762
	Non-Residential	40	$6,922	$14,529

and sizes accounting for a high standard deviation of $10,967. There was less variance in cost per square foot, with libraries on average costing approximately $280 per square foot for new facilities. Table 13 shows general descriptive statistics for the three cost variables. Project costs were not available for one library in the study; this library was therefore removed from the analysis. It was not anticipated that the removal of this library would have too great an impact, as the project was a small addition (<13,000 square feet). Cost was tracked with three distinct variables in this study: overall project cost; cost per square foot; and cost per student. Data on facility cost were derived from project lists in the annual *Bowker Annual of Library and Book Trade Information* as well as a variety of other sources as necessary. These sources included college and university press releases, information from construction companies, library informational resources, and other sources. Research questions associated with this study focused on the relationship of a variety of institutional variables with library cost. The overall goal was to illustrate which institutional variables show correlation with project cost and develop a model that indicates which institutional variables most account for library cost. In other words, what institutional characteristics affect what institutions spend on new library facilities?

Public institutions spent considerably more on average for new library buildings, yet spent three times less per student (see Table 13). Private institutions also spent more per square foot than public institutions, indicating a difference in quality, as there is not a negative correlation between cost per square foot and total cost. Correlation between project cost and whether an institution is public or private is significant at .05; correlation between cost per student and institutional governance is also significant at .01. Finally, while building project cost per student for libraries on residential campuses was only slightly higher than cost per student for new libraries on non-residential campuses, cost per square foot was significantly higher at residential campuses. Table 14 shows differences in costs for new libraries according to institutional setting.

When viewed by enrollment, building project cost and cost per student shows relatively even distribution for both variables across all categories except for special focus institutions, which have significantly greater cost per student for new academic library projects despite far lower average project costs. This finding could primarily be due to the small enrollments at special focus institutions despite a positive and significant correlation ($p<.05$) between enrollment and project cost between these institutions when taken across the entire population (there

TABLE 15 **Comparison of Cost per Student to Build New Libraries by Carnegie Classification**		
Building Project Cost per Student for New Libraries		
Carnegie Classification	N	Average Cost per Student for New Building
Doctoral/Research	32	$2,683.72
Master's	32	$4,531.75
Baccalaureate	29	$9,005.89
Special Focus	6	$32,400.00

were only six special focus institutions in the study population). When controlling for special focus institutions, building project cost per student was highest for libraries at baccalaureate institutions (see Table 15). As a general observation of cost data from Carnegie classification and enrollment profile, there is a relationship between library building project cost per student and exclusively undergraduate institutions. For example, the mean difference between project cost per student for new libraries at baccalaureate institutions and doctoral/research institutions is significant at .05, as is the mean difference between cost per student at exclusively undergraduate institutions and special focus institutions at .05.

The question that remains is what institutional rather than project variables best predict the level of financial investment an institution makes in a new library (one particular project variable, total square footage, while highly correlated with overall costs, is negatively correlated with cost per student and cost per square foot, which is to be expected). Correlation between certain continuous institutional variables and project cost per student were shown to be significant. T-tests for independent samples and one-way ANOVA post hoc tests showed significant mean differences between cost per student across several Carnegie classifications. A significant mean difference was also shown between one enrollment profile, "exclusive graduate professional," and the rest of the enrollment profile groups. However, as there are only four institutions in the enrollment profile variable "exclusive graduate/professional" that account for most of the variance within the five enrollment profiles, controlling for this item eliminates the strength and significance between the enrollment

TABLE 16 **Comparison of Costs to Build New Libraries at Predominately Undergraduate Institutions**			
Building Project Costs for New Libraries at Predominately Undergraduate Institutions			
Public or Private	Enrollment Profile	Cost	Cost per Student
Public	Exclusive Undergraduate*	$26,191,516	$3,634
	Very High Undergraduate*	$24,622,920	$3,587
Private	Exclusive Undergraduate	$14,889,660	$12,458
	Very High Undergraduate	$18,073,314	$9,596

profile and cost per student. The model for the regression analysis for cost per student therefore included the following variables: tuition, enrollment, public/private, Carnegie classification, and enrollment profile. Categorical variables (Carnegie classifications and enrollment profile) were converted to binary numbers in SPSS. The two leading significant predictors for building project cost per student are enrollment, for which there is a negative correlation with lower cost per student to build a new a library as enrollments grow larger; and whether an institution has an exclusively graduate student population, for which there is a positive correlation.

Of the $2.5 billion in new library construction between 2003 and 2009, the average cost per student varied greatly between public and private institutions, with private institutions spending on average three times more per student than public institutions. As with square footage per library building, cost per student may be considered a quality and/or value indicator for the sake of this discussion. At the very least, cost per student provides a measurement of the institution's investment in the new library. Another variable that combines institutional and project data is cost per square foot. Here again, private institutions outspend publics by nearly 25%. As a measure of quality, the differences in cost per student may be better approached by looking not only at the differences between public and private institutions, but also at enrollment profiles and Carnegie classifications. Data from the study of the population indicate that baccalaureate institutions are more likely to spend more money per student on new library buildings than master's and doctoral/research colleges and universities. Using enrollment profile as a guide, the general trend from the population shows that, the greater the undergraduate enrollment level, the higher the cost per student, with the highest cost per student at exclusively undergraduate institutions. It should be noted here that, because the number of undergraduate institutions with exclusively undergraduate and very high undergraduate enrollments in the population is equal for both public and private colleges, one might expect the cost per student at private undergraduate institutions to be much higher.

Participating institutions with exclusively graduate student populations, while small in number, should nonetheless be noted for their significant correlations with more square footage per student and their library building project cost per student. This is most likely due to the fact that special focus institutions are generally private, with low enrollments and very high tuitions (and those in this study were no exception).

In general, then, between 2003 and 2009 there were proportionally (to the population) more libraries being built at institutions with predominately undergraduate enrollments, at a greater cost per student. Based on information gathered in identifying library building projects for the study, numerous new academic libraries, both public and private, emphasize the importance the undergraduate experience in the planning and design of new library space, particularly the social and collaborative aspects of undergraduate learning. Previous studies showed multiuse becoming more common (Shill & Tonner, 2003), which may offer more advantages to undergraduates than graduate students, who use the library space more for collections than space and services (Hiller, 2004). Foote (2004) suggests that library buildings will be judged by an increasing number of criteria. Higher cost per student may well be an expression of the growing trend towards a more multi-varied, multi-functional library, which is an invariably more expensive space than a traditional library designed around print collections and traditional service points.

Comparison of New Library Construction Activity Between 2003–2009 and 1996–2002

Compared to the seven-year period preceding the current study, new library construction has declined by 33%. There were 99 new

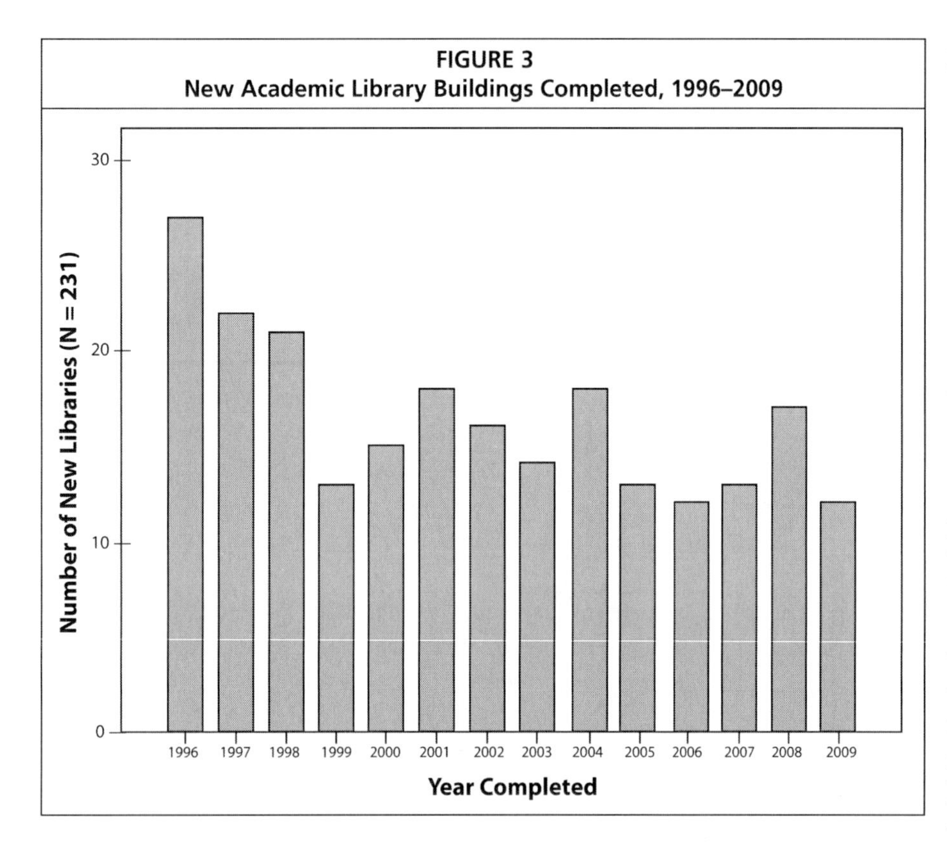

FIGURE 3
New Academic Library Buildings Completed, 1996–2009

academic library buildings completed between 2003 and 2009, compared with 132 projects completed between 1996 and 2002. The number of projects completed for the period 1996-2002 was derived from the annual architecture issues of *American Libraries* and *Library Journal* and then verified in *Bowker Annual of Library and Book Trade Information*, as well as other sources. While it is possible that the current population may not include a small number of library projects, it is also possible that, given the fact that information on older library projects, especially those completed in the previous decade, is more difficult to identify, a larger number of library projects may be missing from the 1996-2002 population. If this is the case, decline in library construction between 2003-2009 and 1996-2002 may be even greater than the data presented here. Therefore, by a conservative estimate, new library construction fell upwards of one third between 2003 and 2009 when compared to the seven-year period between 1996 and 2002. Between 1996 and 2002, an average of 19 new buildings were completed annually, compared to an average of 14 new libraries completed annually between 2003 and 2009. Three of the years between 1996 and 2002 saw more than 20 new academic libraries were completed annually. New academic library construction in 1996 was twice that of new library construction in 2009.

Reasons for this decline in new library construction no doubt stem in part from changing user behavior and information formats, yet cannot be explained by users and institutions moving away from the physical library. This study does not include renovations and smaller additions, for example. As shown in several recently completed, large-scale projects such as the renovated and expanded Thompson Library at Ohio State University, colleges and universities continue to leverage existing space in significant ways. Indeed, library renovation and additions (less than the size of the original structure) listed in the annual architectural issues of *Library Journal* between 1996 and 2009 showed only a modest decrease in activity between 1996-2002 and 2003-2009. However, if one was to assume that investment in new facilities is a bellwether of overall investment in library space across higher education, the argument could be made that the long-term pattern of new academic library construction has been trending downward for some time and is likely to continue in this direction.

One of several explanations for this decline may be found in Hiller's 2004 research at the University of Washington which suggests that, at least for disciplines that are not (or soon not to be) overly dependent on print-based material, library space will gradually lose significance for graduate students and faculty who mainly use the physical library primarily for its collections. Hiller concludes that undergraduates, on the other hand, will continue to use the physical library, primarily for services and the space. Taking Hiller's insights into account, one could theorize that, while investments in departmental and graduate/professional libraries declines as greater portions of information in many disciplines is made available electronically and subject/departmental libraries are consolidated, investment in undergraduate library space has increased in relation to overall construction activity. In proportion to the total number of new libraries built, the percentage of new libraries completed at baccalaureate colleges increased from 17% from 1996-2002 to 29% in 2003-2009. In addition, in proportion to the total number of new libraries built, the percentage of new libraries completed at institutions with more than 90% undergraduate enrollment increased from 22% from 1996 -2002 to 43% in 2003-2009. Finally, despite the fact that there were significantly more buildings completed between 1996 and 2002, the overall number of library buildings completed at institutions with more than 90% undergraduate enrollments (n=33) was higher in the last seven years when compared to 1996-2002.

Summary

Designing this study of new academic library buildings involved identifying numerous institutional and project variables that individually and combined describe what has occurred in academic library construction for the better part of the past decade. This process also involved establishing expected values for the percentage of different types of institutions completing new libraries and the number of these institutions in the overall population of colleges and universities in the United States and it territories.

The average cost to construct a new academic library building was approximately $25 million, with an average cost per student of approximately $7,000. There has been a significant downward trend in new library construction when compared to the seven years prior to this study. While new libraries completed over the past seven years are distributed fairly evenly across private and public institutions as well as residential and non-residential ones, there has been more new library construction at undergraduate institutions over the past seven years than the period prior. There was also high amount of library building activity at public institutions with large undergraduate enrollments, which includes many public, doctoral-granting institutions.

Public institutions completed larger, more expensive library buildings but at a significantly lower cost per student. Institutions with larger enrollments, both public and private, generally spent less per student on new library buildings. As a group, however, private institutions spent significantly more per student on new libraries than public institutions on both residential and non-residential campuses. Most of the private institutions in this study are residential. Residential campus libraries, while smaller, offer far more square feet per student. In general, private institutions build libraries that offer significantly more space per student than public institutions. Differences in institutional investment in library space are not as pronounced, however, between public and private schools with predominately undergraduate populations, which spend more per student on new library space than other enrollment categories.

The study of new academic libraries completed over the past seven years provides a general outline of the level of library building activity as well as the types of institutions completing new libraries. This overview also describes the relationship between numerous institutional variables and the size and cost of new academic library buildings. The next step in gaining a deeper understanding of new academic library physical space in the current era is to explore the factors that motivate planning for these new buildings, how these buildings are designed, and how and how much these new buildings are being used. These questions are addressed in the next phase of this study, a survey sent to leaders at the 99 institutions that completed new academic libraries between 2003 and 2009.

chapter five

RESPONSES TO THE SURVEY

The second phase of this study of academic libraries was a survey sent to each of the 99 libraries completed between 2003 and 2009. The type of data collected from the survey differs from those collected in the first phase of the study. The first phase identified broad institutional and project variables and provided a general overview of academic library construction activity in recent years. The purpose of the survey of the libraries was to gain a deeper understanding of the factors involved in planning new academic libraries, the characteristics and qualities of the facilities, usage, and, to a certain degree, the relationship between traditional library collections and services and the design of these buildings. The three primary research questions concerning planning, space, and usage were addressed through a range of themes, including the library as a learning space, library collections, and functional differences between the old and new library. In addition to quantitative data, respondents were given the opportunity to provide written responses to a number of questions, adding to the depth of data across several areas of the survey.

This chapter will provide a brief summary of methodology, study planning, research design, and methods for analysis. Factors relating to the process of the study will also be discussed, including the role of the first phase of the study in clarifying and verifying data provided by survey respondents. Survey response rates and general characteristics of the sample are also outlined here. In subsequent chapters, findings are discussed in the context of specific themes, beginning with factors involved in planning new libraries.

The sample for this survey was the 58 academic libraries that responded out of the 99 libraries completed between 2003 and 2009 as identified and inventoried in the first phase of this study. The relationship between the overall population of institutions, the group of libraries in the first phase of the study, and the sample is described below:

- Population: 2,267 not-for-profit four-year and above colleges, universities, and special focus institutions in the United States and its territories.
- Subset of the Population: 99 institutions that completed new academic library buildings between 2003 and 2009.
- Sample: 58 institutions that responded to the survey sent to the subset of the population.

Timeframe and Process

Survey design was completed in June 2008. A subset of the population was finalized by August 2008. An email invitation was sent to library deans and directors on August 25, 2008, and the survey period ran through October, 2008. A completed study of new academic library buildings completed between 2003 and 2008 was presented and successfully defended as a doctoral dissertation at the University of Pennsylvania Graduate School of Education in spring, 2009. As the research was being prepared for publication as a book, the decision was made to extend the study an additional year to include libraries completed in 2009. In January, 2010, the survey was subsequently sent to library directors at institutions that completed and opened new buildings through the end of 2009. Completed surveys were received through February, 2010. This survey invitation message was personalized to address library directors by surname as well as to identify the specific new building project at his or her institution. The message then described the purpose and significance of the study, invited participation, provided a link to the web survey, and assured confidentiality.

In both the 2008 and 2009 survey periods, reminders were sent at two-week intervals only to those institutions that had not yet responded. The majority of responses came back in the first week of the survey periods. A handful of libraries were eliminated from the subset and sample because, in review of survey results, it was concluded that they did not meet the criteria for inclusion. In the final analysis, 58 libraries out of the 99 libraries completed between 2003 and 2009 completed surveys, representing an overall response rate of 59%. Data transfer from the survey to Microsoft Excel took place in December 2008 and again in March, 2010. Data were imported into SPSS (v.16) for statistical analysis.

Findings and Discussion

The 99 institutions that built new libraries between 2003 and 2009 included colleges, universities, and institutes of all Carnegie classes and enrollment profiles used as criteria to identify and categorize institutions in the first phase of this study. Survey responses came from libraries across all years of the study, although responses from libraries completed in 2006 and 2009 were low, as may be expected given that those years saw the lowest construction activity in the study's seven-year period.

TABLE 17
Responses to the Survey of New Academic Library Buildings, 2003–2009 (n = 58)

Year Completed	Frequency	Percent	Cumulative Percent
2003	8	14	14
2004	9	16	30
2005	11	19	48
2006	5	9	57
2007	9	16	72
2008	11	19	91
2009	5	9	100
Total	58	100	

TABLE 18
Survey Respondents by Carnegie Classification (n = 58)

	Frequency	Percent	Expected Value (%)
Baccalaureate	15	26	29
Master's	26	45	33
Doctoral/Research	14	24	29
Special Focus	3	5	5
Total	58	100	100

Institutional Factors and New Academic Library Buildings

In general, the survey sample is representative of the population subset of 99 institutions that completed new library buildings between 2003 and 2009. Fifty-three percent of the survey respondents were public institutions, compared with 51% of all institutions that built new libraries. Similarly, 47% of the survey respondents in to the survey were private institutions, versus 49% in the population of institutions that completed new li-

TABLE 19
Survey Respondents by Institutional Setting (n = 58)

	Frequency	Percent	Expected Value (%)
Residential	39	67	60
Non-Residential	19	33	40
Total	58	100	100

TABLE 20 Survey Respondents by Institutional Setting, Governance, and Enrollment Profile								
		Enrollment Profile*						
		EXU	VHU	HU	MU	MGP	EXGP	Total
Public	Residential	1	6	7	1			15
		2%	10%	12%	2%			26%
	Non-Residential	6	6	4	7	1		24
		10%	10%	7%	12%	2%		41%
	Total	7	12	11	8	1		39
		12%	20%	19%	14%	2%		67%
Private	Residential	2	4	8	2			16
		3%	7%	14%	3%			28%
	Non-Residential	0	0	0	0		3	3
		.0%	.0%	.0%	.0%		5%	5%
	Total	2	4	8	2		3	19
		3%	7%	14%	3%		5%	33%

EXU=Exclusively Undergraduate; VHU=Very High Undergraduate; HU=High Undergraduate; MU=Majority Undergraduate; MGP=Majority Graduate; EXGP=Exclusively Graduate/Professional

brary buildings. Expected values for residential institutions versus non-residential institutions also closely approximated the study population. Table 18 lists expected values for residential versus non-residential colleges and universities based on the 99 institutions that completed new library buildings between 2003 and 2009.

Variables related to Carnegie classification and institutional enrollment profiles distributed slightly unevenly between the study population subset and the survey respondents, although the differences were not major. Expected values for the sample based on the population of institutions that completed new libraries did not deviate markedly in any Carnegie classification. For Carnegie classification (see Table 18), 45% (26) of the libraries responding to the survey are included in the masters colleges and universities group, versus 33% (n=33) in the subset of population, representing a 79% response rate for institutions in this Carnegie category. For doctoral/research universities, however, 29% (n=14), the survey response rate was only 45%. As with the study population subset, however, expected values for survey responses for doctoral/research universities that answered surveys far exceeded the percentage of these institutions in the overall population 2,267 not-for-profit four-year and above colleges, universities, and special focus institutions in the United States and its territories (29% versus 12% in the overall population).

Institutional representation according to enrollment profile among the survey respondents closely approximated the population of institutions completing new libraries—with the exception of institutions with majority graduate student enrollments (of the four institutions in of this category in the subset, only one was represented in the survey respondents). The highest number of responses came from libraries at institutions described as having exclusive or very high undergraduate populations. Table 20 contains cross-tabulations of enrollment profile and institutional setting for the survey sample. It shows that, across categories, public colleges and universities with majority to exclusive undergraduate populations represented the largest number of survey respondents, which approximates the population of institutions that built new libraries. These institutions are often doctoral research universities with large undergraduate populations. None of the survey respondents were private, non-residential institutions, reflecting the very small number of private, non-residential institutions overall that built new academic libraries.

Conclusion

The goal of the survey was to gather data on characteristics of new library space, how these spaces are used, and primary factors that inform the planning of these buildings. From a study population subset of 99 institutions that completed new academic library buildings between 2003 and 2009, the survey response rate was 59%. Responses generally approximated expected values based on the study population, with the majority of responses coming from institutions with large undergraduate populations. The fewest number of responses came from libraries completed in 2006 and 2009. In general, then, it can be assumed that survey data that will be presented in coming chapters is representative of libraries used by undergraduate student populations. We will begin the discussion of survey results with an analysis of planning factors for new academic libraries.

chapter six

PLANNING NEW LIBRARY BUILDINGS

One of the primary goals of this study was to identify major factors that inform planning for new library buildings. Respondents were asked the age of the building being replaced. Additionally, respondents were asked if the building being replaced would be used for another purpose and what that purpose would be. Respondents were also asked whether environmental concerns were a part of planning for the new facility—specifically whether sustainable materials and technology were incorporated into the design of the new facility. Participants were also asked to identify funding sources for their new libraries. Finally, participants were asked to rank level of motivation for 16 distinct planning considerations ranging from growth of collections to obsolescence of the building's mechanical systems. This list of planning factors was partially derived from a previous survey instrument (Bennett, 2003), as well as discussions with other researchers from previous studies. Participants were given the chance to provide additional responses via a semi-closed question on planning factors at the end of the section.

Age of Buildings Being Replaced

The most common age range for library buildings that were replaced or added to was 25 to 49 years (see Table 21). Nearly 60% of libraries responding to the survey fell into this group. The overwhelming majority of respondents also reported that the old facility was not torn down. Forty-six of the 58 survey participants offered additional information on how the old facility was being used. A small number of those reported that the old facility remained as part of a renovated and expanded library complex. A larger number of respondents reported that the old facility was being re-commissioned as administrative

TABLE 21
Age of Library Buildings Being Replaced by New Library (n = 58)

	Frequency	Percent	Valid Percent	Cumulative Percent
Old Building Not Replaced	4	6.9	7.5	7.5
Less than 25 Years	7	12.1	13.2	20.8
25-49 Years	31	53.4	58.5	79.2
50-74 Years	5	8.6	9.4	88.7
75-99 Years	3	5.2	5.7	94.3
More than 100 Years	3	5.2	5.7	100.0
Total	53	92.5	100.0	
Missing		5	8.6	
Total	58	100.0		

TABLE 22
Planning Considerations for New Library Buildings

Which of the following considerations motivated your library building project? Please indicate the strength of motivation for as many considerations that apply. Use the last column to indicate the consideration was not a factor.

Answer Options	Strong Motivation		Intermediate Motivation		Weak Motivation	N/A	Rating Average	Response Count
Growth of library staff (either librarians or support staff)	1	6	8	4	27	10	1.98	56
Increase in number of library service points	0	1	9	9	20	16	1.41	55
Growth of the collections	21	18	5	2	7	3	3.83	56
Changing character of student body space needs	33	12	7	1	1	3	4.35	57
Change in reference services	5	2	18	7	16	8	2.13	56
Changes in public services other than circulation (e.g., ILL)	3	8	10	11	11	13	2.56	56
Changes in information technology	35	11	6	1	2	3	4.38	58
Changes in technical services and other library operations with little interactions with library users	0	1	8	12	21	13	1.95	55
Preservation of the collections	7	13	16	8	10	3	2.98	57
Need to accommodate operations not previously housed in the library (e.g., computing centers; general classrooms or offices)	20	7	12	3	6	9	3.67	57
Aesthetic considerations and creature comfort	27	12	8	2	3	3	4.12	55
Building safety issues	9	11	9	11	6	10	3.13	56
Mechanical systems obsolescence	14	11	8	7	9	7	3.25	56
Requirements of the Americans with Disabilities Act	8	11	12	6	13	7	2.90	57
Building structural problems (including earthquake protection)	6	11	7	3	16	13	2.72	56
Dysfunctional design of previous space	19	15	6	3	8	4	3.67	55
Other considerations (please describe)								24

and/or academic space for the university. By far this was the most common reported use of the old library building. Finally, four respondents reported that the old library building was to be renovated into a student center, while one former library building has seen new life as a fitness center.

Sources of Funding for New Library Buildings

Fifty-four of the 58 respondents provided information on funding sources for their new library buildings. The most commonly reported funding source was state/government funding, with nearly two-thirds of respondents reporting that their projects were at least in part funded in this manner. In total, half of the respondents indicated that their projects were at least in part funded via a fundraising campaign. Three respondents added that the library was the highlight of an institutional campaign. Of the respondents that reported that their library projects were funded via an institutional campaign, eight indicated funding from a library-only development campaign. Seven respondents reported that most or the majority of funds for the new facility came from one or two major donors or deceased alumni.

Bazillion and Braun (2001) expect many new libraries in the current era to be in service 100 years from now. Data from the current study show that libraries in the previous era did not enjoy that kind of staying power. In fact, two-thirds of survey respondents reported that the average age of the library being replaced with a new facility was between 25 and 49 years old, comparatively young by academic architecture standards. Moreover, an additional 21% of respondents indicated that the building being replaced was less than 25 years old. As the population of the current study included only new buildings or significant additions, it is assumed that the old space was outmoded as a library facility due to a variety of shortcomings. However, this is not to say that most of old library buildings were torn down. As previously mentioned, many found new life as academic and administrative buildings—testaments to the rapidly changing, increasingly complex demands of the academic library space compared to the relative simplicity of office and classroom facilities. Sustainable architecture and integration with the surrounding natural setting were also identified by many libraries as important design considerations. Respondents also reported heavy use of natural light in the new facilities, which indicates that traditional print collections are being housed away from the most frequented areas of the new building.

Planning Factors for New Academic Library Buildings

Respondents ranked the importance of 16 planning considerations, many derived from a previous survey instrument (Bennett, 2003) along a scale of "strong motivation" to "weak motivation" (N/A was also included). Numerically, these responses translated into 5 (strong motivation) to 3 (intermediate motivation) to 1 (weak motivation). Survey participants ranked each of the 16 planning motivators. "Changing character of study body space needs" and "changes in information technology" were the highest ranked planning factors with nearly equal average rating scores of 4.35 (n=57) and 4.38 (n=58), respectively. "Aesthetic considerations and creature comforts" was the third highest planning factor with a mean score of 4.12 (n=55). Remaining considerations that received the most responses as strong planning considerations were poor design of the previous space; mechanical systems obsolescence; growth of the collections; and need to accommodate non-library space into the new building. Growth of the collections ranked fourth overall with a rating average of 3.83.

Factors that had little or no role in planning the new building were primarily related to library operations and more traditional functions. For example, only one respondent identified "growth in library staff" as a strong planning factor, while 32 respondents listed this as either a weak or non-applicable planning factor. Similarly, no respondents identified increasing the number of service points in the library as a strong planning factor, while 37 respondents considered this factor either a weak motivator or not applicable. "Increasing the number of library service points" received the lowest average (1.41) of the 16 planning considerations. Changes in public services and changes in non-public service library operations received each received 13 "N/A" responses and lackluster rating averages. Changes in reference services ranked similarly low with a rating average of 2.13. Planning considerations and accompanying scores are included in Table 22.

Respondents were also given the opportunity to provide additional information on planning factors through a semi-closed question. Twenty-seven respondents did so. While no single theme emerged from these responses, several topics arose and were shared among groups. The first of these was accreditation. Several libraries reported that one of the primary planning motivators was to build a larger space to meet accreditation standards for square footage and study space and/or to meet growing enrollments. One respondent described the situation plainly—"accreditation recommendation stated that old library size was inadequate"—but added that in planning for the new library the university would emphasize the "image of the new building" as a "recruiting and retention issue." Another planning consideration that was common among several respondents was the strong desire to incorporate new and/or expanded learning space in response to the evolving role of the academic library. One respondent put it thusly:

> The basic function of libraries has changed from being a warehouse for books to a place for human interaction and learning. This was the prime motivation for designing the new space.

A handful of respondents reported that primary planning for the new library was part of a move to an entirely new campus or a final move from a temporary library space. For both groups, the new library's physical presence on the new campus was considered a major element in campus design. One respondent indicated that planning was motivated by a need to consolidate collections and several branch libraries. Finally, a small group of libraries, likely expanding on the question regarding the incorporation of non-library units in the new facility, described organizational imperatives such as the "need to combine library and IT services" and co-locate staff from "different campus information services/resources to enhance collaboration *among* these staff and *between* them and faculty."

Bennett's (2003) study of libraries completed between 1992 and 2001 found that growth of library collections heavily influenced the library planning process. In his study, growth of collections was the "strongest project motivator" among the majority of the 220 responding libraries. In the current survey of academic library projects completed between 2003 and 2009, however, growth of library collections was *not* identified by respondents as the strongest planning motivator. The leading planning motivators identified by respondents in the current study were "changing character of student body space needs," and "changes in information technology" with roughly 60% of the respondents identifying both as strong motivators in planning new library buildings. In Bennett's study, only 45% of respondents reported "changing character of student body space needs" as a strong planning motivator. One of several planning motivators added to the current study, "aesthetic considerations and creature comforts," was rated as a strong motivator by 50% of respondents. This change in ranking of factors motivating planning for new libraries represents a shift in the current era. Both Freeman (2005) and Bennett (2003, 2005) argue that libraries should be planned around student learning. The library building is evolving from a collections-centered space to a multi-varied, multi-functional space. Interestingly, as the library transforms into a more student and service-oriented facility, operational concerns such as increasing the number of service points in the building were identified as having little influence on the planning process. Yet, as will be discussed later, the majority of libraries in the current study reported increases in staff areas and service points in the new building.

Modern Library Planning: Implications for Physical Collections

Results from the current study reveal trends in how new libraries are storing and providing access to print collections. By including only new academic library buildings, this study provides a clearer picture of how library leaders plan and manage collections without the encumbrance of legacy buildings and often-retrofitted space. By asking survey participants a series of questions about library collections, this study sought to assess the impact both traditional print and digital collections play in new library buildings. Questions ranged from those covering general characteristics such as collection size to questions about anticipated growth (or shrinkage) of print collections as well as physical space planning for books in the coming decades.

As discussed earlier, results data showed a lessening of priority for physical collections as a factor in space planning when compared to libraries built in the previous decade. This study also explored several other dimensions of the role print collections play in new academic library space, including level of acquisitions, storage of material, and use of traditional collections. In part, this study extends Shill and Tonner's (2003) investigation of the importance of print collections in new academic libraries. In addition to continuing selected questions from the earlier study, the current study also introduced a set of new questions that allowed respondents to describe, in their own words, factors that will affect acquiring and managing print collections in these new libraries in the coming years.

Using the National Center on Educational Statistics (NCES) definition for physical collections as a guide, respondents (n=54) indicated a wide range of collection sizes. A handful of libraries in the sample housed less than 50,000 volumes, while two libraries reported collection sizes in excess of 4 million volumes. A majority of libraries reported collection sizes between 100,000 and 249,000 (n=14) and 250,000 and 499,000 (n=13). Nine libraries indicated a volume count between 1,000,000 and 2,999,999.

As many librarians and researchers have stressed the importance of onsite access to collections as an important part of learning, this survey asked respondents to indicate how much of their physical collections are located in open stacks; compact shelving; automatic storage and retrieval systems (ASRS); and offsite. Thirty-six libraries, or 65% of respondents, indicated that between 91% and 100% of their collections were browsable in open stacks. Cross-tabs showed a general pattern of higher percentages of collections in open stacks at baccalaureate institutions. While several libraries at master's and doctoral institutions indicated less than 50% of their collections were available in open stacks, no baccalaureate institutions indicated less than 50% of their collections were in open stacks, and only one indicated that between 91% and 100% of their physical collection were *not* in open stacks. While undergraduate institutions in this study showed higher percentages of collections in open stacks, many of the institutions with higher percentages of collections in open stacks also reported static or declining acquisition rates for book collections. Rate of growth in print collections will be discussed later.

Responses indicated that a good number of new libraries are incorporating compact shelving into new facilities. Well over half of respondents (n=33) indicated that they used compact

TABLE 23
Annual Rate of Growth of Print Collections for New Academic Libraries (n = 58)

	Frequency	Percent	Valid Percent	Cumulative Percent
Number of Volumes Added is Increasing	23	39.7	41.1	41.1
Number of Volumes Added Remains Static	22	37.9	39.3	80.4
Number of Volumes Added is Declining	11	19.0	19.6	100.0
Total	56	96.6	100.0	
Missing	2	3.4		
Total	58	100.0		

shelving in the new library. Of these, more than a third indicated less than 10% of the collection was stored in compact shelving, eight libraries indicated between 10% and 24%; six libraries indicated between 25% and 49% in compact shelving; three libraries reported between 50% and 74% of collections in compact shelving; and three libraries indicated between 75% and 99% of collections in compact shelving. Compact shelving was included in new library space with far more frequency than the more expensive automatic storage retrieval systems (ASRSs). Six libraries reported using robotic systems, but of these, the majority stored significant portions (25%-74%) of their collections in these systems. Libraries using ASRSs are generally larger than libraries using compact shelving that house most of their collections in open stacks. Libraries using robotic systems for collections were an average of 199,333 square feet in size, versus an average of 96,685 square feet for other libraries in the study. As more libraries implement ASRSs in coming years, a larger sample will become available to determine if these systems are most common in larger academic libraries. In this study, four of the libraries using these systems rank among the top 10 largest academic libraries built in the last six years. Three of these libraries were completed in 2008. Finally, 10 libraries reported having offsite storage facilities. As expected, the majority of these libraries are doctoral/research universities with large research collections and a large amount of older material. Half of the libraries with offsite storage indicated that between 10% and 24% percent of their collections are housed offsite.

Use of compact shelving by more than 50% of the new libraries in the study is consistent with results from Shill and Tonner's (2003) study and indicates a continued preference for storage systems that allow for at least partial browsing. Demas (2005) argues for the value of serendipity as a "common and treasured experience in libraries," and offers that building expansion and compact shelving allow colleges to keep as much of their collections as possible on campus, preserving the possibility for serendipity in the stacks. Crawford (1999) stresses the value of the book, as it requires "time on task" learning and aids intellectual development. The value of serendipity and local access to print collections is in part reflected in the inclusion of compact storage in new libraries rather than offsite facilities. In these new buildings, however, larger percentages of the collection are being stored in compact shelving, with approximately 25% of libraries using compact shelving systems to store 10% to 24% of their collections.

Shill and Tonner's (2003) study also showed only two libraries using ASRSs, while six libraries in the current study reported using such systems. Given that the current study comprised a smaller sample than the Shill and Tonner study, one may conclude that the growth of storage retrieval systems is a gradually developing trend in new academic library spaces. The least likely compromise appears to be offsite storage, with a lower percentage of libraries in the current study reporting that they use such facilities. These results may be in part due to the fact that the sample included only new library buildings that can accommodate growing collections. However, the continued preference for compact shelving and the growing use of ASRSs indicate that new libraries are addressing current as well as anticipated storage needs onsite. Hickey (2001), however, warns that, as more libraries move materials offsite and into local in-house storage systems, the material will inevitably be used less, creating a caste system that favors newer print and digital resources. Other studies have shown that students associate printed material with higher quality research (Dilevko & Gottleib, 2002). The continued growth of automatic storage and retrieval systems and growing preference towards open user space over open stacks reveal how library planners think about the level of compromise users are willing to accept for access to physical collections.

Another indicator of the level of priority placed on books in the new library space is the percentage of the collection that remains in open stacks. Seen through the lens of enrollment, the percentage of collections in open stacks in these new libraries is higher at undergraduate colleges and master's colleges and universities. While it is true that undergraduate and master's institutions are likely to have smaller collections than doctoral/research institutions, this is not always the case. Moreover, library floor space, even in new, larger facilities, is always at a premium, especially given the growing trend towards multiuse. Higher percentages of collections in open stacks at undergraduate and master's institutions in this study may offer some insight into the continued value of book collections in support of undergraduate learning. When one accounts for the number of volumes these new libraries are acquiring, however, the issue becomes more layered (see Table 24). The majority of libraries reporting static levels of print acquisition report between 91% and 100% of collections in open stacks, which seems to indicate that a lack of shelf space is unrelated to the pullback in book buying. Similarly, half of the libraries reporting declining print acquisitions also reported between 91% and 100% of their collections being stored in open stacks.

Growth of print collections remains an important although not necessarily primary consideration in academic library planning. A study of libraries built between 1995 and 2002 (Shill & Tonner, 2003) explored how print collection growth was planned in new academic library space by asking respondents to indicate when they expected shelving capacity in their new facility to be exhausted. Approximately one third of the respondents indicated that their libraries were prepared to accommodate growth in print collections for the next two or more decades. However, another third of respondents indicated that shelf space would be exhausted in the coming decade. In the current study, roughly a third of respondents indicated that the new building could accommodate collections beyond 2031; another third indicated space for collection growth beyond 2021 and, like the earlier study, nearly a third indicated space for collections could not accommodate growth beyond the next decade. There are significant positive correlations between library project cost ($p<.01$), total square footage ($p<.01$), and cost per square foot ($p<.05$) and libraries reporting exhausting space for print collections after 2031, indicating that larger, more expensive libraries are likely to be more prepared for long-term growth of print collections. The majority of these libraries are part of public universities.

Two remaining questions about planning for print collections asked respondents to describe the rate of growth of their print collections and to identify the three most important factors affecting planning for print collection growth in the com-

TABLE 24 Annual Rate of Print Growth Collection and Percentage of Collection in Open Stacks					
	Percentage of Collection in Open Stacks				
	<50%	50%–70%	75%–90%	91%–100%	Total
Acquisitions Increasing	1	1	6	15	23
	4.3%	4.3%	26.1%	65.2%	100.0%
Acquisitions Remains Static	1	1	4	16	22
	4.5%	4.5%	18.2%	72.7%	100.0%
Acquisitions Decreasing	3	2	0	5	10
	30.0%	20.0%	.0%	50.0%	100.0%
Total	5	4	10	36	55
	9.1%	7.3%	18.2%	65.5%	100.0%

ing years. Forty percent (n=22) of respondents reported that the number of volumes added to the print collection each year remains static, and 19% (n=10) reported that the amount of print material acquired each year is declining. Data comparing print acquisitions and enrollment illustrates an unsettling link between size of a library's print collections and the number of students enrolled at the institution. Libraries that reported annual growth of the print collections had on average far smaller enrollments than libraries at institutions that reported static growth of the collections and significantly smaller enrollments (in terms of mean difference) than libraries that reported declining print acquisitions. A one-way ANOVA test showed that there is significant difference between enrollment means at schools whose libraries reported annual increases in the number of print volumes acquired and those who reported the number of print volumes to be decreasing. The average enrollment was 14,748 students at institutions with libraries reporting declining print acquisitions; 9,416 students at institutions whose libraries reported static growth in print collections; and 5,820 at institutions reporting the number of print volumes increasing each year. Taken in terms of Carnegie classifications, the majority of libraries reporting static or declining growth in their print collections were at public master's and doctoral/research institutions. Larger institutions, including several doctoral/re-

TABLE 25 Rate of Growth of Print Collections and Enrollment		
Annual Rate of Growth of Print Collection	Number of Institutions	Average Enrollment
Rate of Added Volumes is Increasing	23	5,820
Rate of Added Volumes Remains Static	22	9,416
Rate of Added Volumes is Decreasing	11	14,748

search universities with more students (including, assumedly, sizable undergraduate populations) would presumably require larger print collections, but are more likely to be maintaining current levels or even reducing the size of their print collections. Roughly the same percentage (38%) of institutions reported growth of print acquisitions as reported static levels of acquisitions at institutions with majority to exclusively undergraduate enrollments. All of the institutions reporting declining levels of print acquisition were at institutions with majority to exclusively undergraduate populations.

Respondents overwhelmingly listed the increasing availability of online library resources as the most important factor affecting collection development in the coming years. Respondents described the situation in a variety of ways, but with common language such as "e-resources" and "electronic availability." Some respondents indicated that planning for collections would also include digital monographs as e-book platforms gain acceptance. After online resources, the second most frequently mentioned factor affecting collection planning was budget, followed by curriculum. Curriculum was listed in a range of contexts, including the expansion of graduate programs, "teaching thrusts," and the library's role in supporting an institution's liberal arts mission.

Given data from the survey on anticipated shelf space exhaustion in combination with data on rates of collection growth, it may not be surprising that physical space was identified by only a handful of respondents as a factor in planning for print collections. With nearly two-thirds of respondents reporting either static or declining acquisitions, there was a definite trend among the libraries in this study towards a slowing in the rate of annual book purchasing. How these libraries plan for print collections was also investigated by asking respondents to indicate when they expected space for their print collections to be exhausted. When compared to Shill and Tonner's (2003) study and Hickey's (2001) assertion that many libraries are not making predictions for print collections beyond 15 years, results of the current study indicated that the majority of libraries completed between 2003 and 2009 are equipped to accommodate print collections in the long-term. Capacity may not be predicated by new acquisitions alone, however, but also by a reduction of print collections in the long term when one accounts for the weeding out of old, outdated, and damaged materials and, of course, declining book purchasing overall. In other words, libraries may not be planning for accommodating print collections because they expect the problem to solve itself.

Many continue to make the case for the long-term viability of print collections for academic libraries. Walters (2008) argues that the "book centered" collection remains a far more economically sustainable, effective learning resource that is "consistent with the goals of many undergraduate colleges" (p. 576). Supply and demand also factors into the equation. While digitization of journals and reference material is a foregone conclusion in many disciplines, especially across many of the sciences, medicine, engineering, and law, the printed monograph remains well-represented across most subjects. There were 77,534 scholarly titles published in North America in 2006 versus 75,384 in 2005 and 60,111 in 2004 (Morrow, 2008). Mann (2001) declares that the book remains the library's most vital asset.

Still, it is clear from the survey data that, at least partially, book collections will continue to be affected by the availability of material in digital formats. This effect on print collections may occur through a diversion of resources away from the book budget towards electronic databases and journals, which are often no less expensive and often more expensive than the print versions. There are also several non-space factors affecting the way librarians approach acquisitions. Some of these factors, such as supporting the curriculum, are long established and straightforward. Others, such as the suitability of digital formats over print, are more complex and likely to be resolved at the subject level. Whatever the case, the continued use of compact shelving and ASRSs and the availability of electronic resources are extending library shelf space by many years, allowing for more long-range planning. Current and anticipated cuts in the rate of growth of print collections, likely unpopular in many academic circles but obviously already occurring, may also result in extended storage capacity in the coming years, provided the space is not claimed for other uses. Finally, use (circulation) of print collections in new library facilities was not investigated in this study, so observations cannot be made on the relationships between variables such as building use and use of the collections.

Conclusion

The section of the survey devoted to planning issues involved in new libraries showed that many new buildings are being constructed to replace facilities that did not have very long lives as library buildings. In general, former library buildings are not being torn down, but refitted for use as non-library academic, administrative, and student space. The most common source of funding for new library buildings was public monies, while approximately 25% of projects were funded through development campaigns and/or private gifts. The strongest planning motivators for new library buildings were the changing nature of needs of the student body for library space and changes in information technology—rather than growth of physical collections. Most libraries reported a preference for shelving and storage systems that enabled physical collections to remain onsite and browsable. The higher the undergraduate population, the higher the percentage of collections reported to be housed in open stacks in the new library building. However, nearly two-thirds of libraries responding to the survey reported static or declining levels of acquisition for print materials. Institutions with smaller enrollments were most likely to report growing levels of print acquisition, while institutions with larger enrollments and larger library facilities were most likely to report declining levels of print acquisitions. While libraries are getting larger but print acquisition stagnant or declining, it is fair to assume that growth of physical collections will continue to recede as a motivator for building new library buildings. The library space is changing rapidly. The next chapter will describe some of the primary characteristics of these new library buildings.

chapter seven

CHARACTERISTICS OF NEW LIBRARY BUILDINGS

Size of New Libraries

Of the 58 libraries completing the survey, the average building size was approximately 110,074 square feet. There was a wide array of building sizes, ranging from the smallest facility at 7,000 square feet to the largest, a mixed public-academic library at a large state university, at 475,000 square feet. As with the subset of the population described in chapter four, significant correlations were shown at the .05 level between library square footage and the following institutional variables: cost per student tuition and fees, and enrollment. Significant correlations at the .01 level are shown between square footage and total project cost. Cross-tabs revealed larger libraries were far more common at public universities. Again, these results closely approximate findings from the 99 libraries in the subset of the population.

The largest libraries among the survey sample were grouped in the doctoral/research university Carnegie classification, with an average size of 139,161 square feet. The smallest libraries were found among specialty institutions. When grouped with enrollment profiles, the largest libraries were found at institutions with very high and high undergraduate student populations (presumably also doctoral granting), while the smallest facilities were grouped in exclusively graduate and exclusively undergraduate institutions.

New academic libraries are larger, often significantly so, than the buildings they extended or replaced altogether. Fifty-five of the responses to this question indicated that the new facility was larger than the old. These data compare and extend results from Shill and Tonner's (2003) study, which found significant increases in the size of new library buildings. Because the sample generally approximated the subset of the population, significant correlations between building size and an institution's public or private status and overall project costs are believed to exist among libraries in the survey as well.

This exploration of library size also provided evidence of the continuing trend towards multiuse new buildings. Both Shill and Tonner (2003) and Freeman (2005) discuss multiuse using data

TABLE 26
Library Square Footage by Enrollment Profile

Enrollment Profile	Average Square Footage	N	Standard Deviation
Exclusive Undergraduate	72,343	9	42,200
Very High Undergraduate	110,573	16	55,236
High Undergraduate	146,265	19	120,431
Majority Undergraduate	100,250	10	46,354
Majority Graduate/Professional	71,500	1	
Exclusive Graduate/Professional	37,017	3	33,315
Total	107,739	58	85,143

TABLE 27 Percentage of New Library Facilities Designated for Library-Use Only (n = 58)			
	Frequency	Percent	Cumulative Percent
Less than 50%	7	12.1	12.3
50%–74%	12	20.7	33.3
75%–99%	30	51.7	86
100%	8	13.8	100.0
Total	57	98.3	
Missing	1	1.9	
Total	58	100.0	

and examples. Approximately 33% of the respondents in Shill and Tonner's study indicated that 100% of the new building was designated for library-only purposes. Only 14% (n=8) of the respondents in the current study indicated that 100% of the library was designated for library use only. In general, the amount of space designated for library use only increases with the number of undergraduates enrolled. As the results indicate, institutions with majority or exclusively graduate student populations allocate less space in the new building for library use only. While the number of institutions in the survey with exclusive graduate student populations was too small to generalize, it seems plausible that, given the fact that many institutions with exclusively graduate student populations (e.g., institutes) are located in single buildings that

TABLE 28 Percentage of New Library Designated for Library-Use and Institutional Enrollment Profile					
Enrollment Profile	Less than 50%	50%–74%	75%–99%	100%	Total
Exclusively Undergraduate	0	2	4	2	8
	0%	25.0%	50.0%	25.0%	100.0%
Very High Undergraduate	2	2	10	2	16
	12.5%	12.5%	62.5%	12.5%	100.0%
High Undergraduate	1	6	10	2	19
	5.3%	31.6%	52.6%	10.5%	100.0%
Majority Undergraduate	1	1	6	2	10
	.0%	12.5%	62.5%	25.0%	100.0%
Majority Graduate	0	1	0	0	1
	.0%	100.0%	.0%	.0%	100.0%
Exclusively Graduate/Professional	3	0	0	0	3
	100.0%	.0%	.0%	.0%	100.0%
Total	7	12	30	8	57
	12.3%	21.1%	52.6%	14.0%	100.0%

house a mix of academic and administrative offices, it is common for library space to be shared as well.

Multiuse

It has become more common for academic libraries to share space with non-library functions. The question becomes not if this is occurring, but at what measure. Approximately 53% (n=30) of libraries in the survey reported that between 75% and 99% of the new space was designed for library purposes only, while approximately 14% (n=8) reported that 100% of the new space was designated for library use only. Only seven libraries out of the 57 respondents to this question reported less than half of the new space was designated for library use only. A cross-tab analysis shows that the majority of institutions with exclusive or very high undergraduate populations reported between 75% and 100% of the new facility designated for library use only. While mixed use of the library space has become more common, as will be discussed later, higher percentages of undergraduates tends to translate into less of the new building being used for non-library purposes. While the number of institutions with majority and exclusively graduate student populations in this study is small, it is interesting to note that none of the new libraries at these institutions reported more than 74% of the space designated for library use only. The two exclusively graduate institutions reported less than 50% of the new library space for library purposes only.

TABLE 29
Non-Library Facilities Included in Old and New Library

Non-Library Facility	Old Facility	New Facility	Response Count
General computer lab(s)	57.7% (26)	95.5% (43)	45
Snack bar or cafe	15.2% (7)	97.8% (45)	46
General use classrooms	37.8% (14)	97.2% (36)	37
Conference/meeting rooms	44.0% (22)	100.0% (50)	50
Auditorium	23.0% (3)	100.0% (13)	13
Tutoring center	21.0% (4)	89.4% (17)	19
Writing center	18.1% (4)	95.4% (21)	22
Archives	68.1% (30)	88.6% (39)	44
Bookstore	40.0% (2)	100.0% (5)	5
Copy center	73.7% (14)	94.7% (18)	19
Academic department(s)	90.0% (9)	60.0% (6)	10
Art gallery or museum space	27.6% (8)	89.7% (26)	29
Other (please describe)			22
Answered question			56
Skipped question			2

Respondents were asked to identify non-library facilities in the new building versus the old facility. Respondents identified a wide range of non-library facilities in the new space that were not included in the old library or, if they were, were greatly expanded in the new building. Data were provided by 56 of the 58 of survey respondents. Non-library facilities increased significantly in new libraries. In some cases, these facilities existed in the old structures, but in many more instances, they were newly incorporated. For example, 26 libraries reported having general computer labs in the old building versus 43 in the new library. Cafes were included in 45 new libraries versus only seven of the old facilities, and bookstores were included in five new libraries. Conference rooms and collaborative space also increased significantly, with 50 libraries reporting that these functions were included in the new building. Classrooms and auditoriums also increased in the new buildings, as did some of the non-library facilities that are generally more common in today's academic library, including tutoring and writing centers, university archives, and art galleries. Indeed, art galleries and museum space saw significant increases in new libraries, with nearly half of the libraries in the survey reporting having these spaces in the new building versus only a handful of libraries with art galleries and museum space existing before new construction. Table 29 lists these facilities and number of respondents per type of facility function.

Respondents were also given the opportunity to describe non-library facilities not listed in the questionnaire. Of the 23 that did so, several described the inclusion of IT helpdesks as well as media labs. Several respondents described the addition of centers for assisting faculty and graduate students in developing digital content material for their courses. Other faculty-centered space identified by respondents included a "Faculty Innovation Center" and a "Center for Teaching Excellence."

In decades past, faculty and students (and, of course, librarians themselves) were unlikely to identify spaces and services that were not related to physical collections as within the library's areas of expertise and responsibility. Over the past few decades, however, those distinctions have become far less clear and, in the current era, have become even less so. Meeting rooms, computer labs, and classrooms have become integral to the library's function, and could be considered essential elements of the library space. Indeed, in this study as well as Shill and Tonner's study, these spaces were considered library facilities so long as they were designated primarily for library use. However, elements such as conference rooms, art galleries, non-library classrooms and computer labs, and coffee bars were considered non-library facilities in the current survey, as they have been in previous studies. The inclusion of these kinds of facilities in new libraries reflects the evolution of the library's role in institutional life.

As general-use classroom and computer lab space remain at a premium on most campuses, it is perhaps no surprise that these facilities are the most likely included in new library designs. Coffee bars and cafes were also reported in far higher percentages than earlier studies, as were conference rooms and other collaborative space, all of which indicate the continuing emergence of the library as a multipurpose destination. To that point, while more than half of the libraries in the current study reported the inclusion of art galleries and/or museum spaces in the new building, only a handful of libraries completed between 1997 and 2002 included art galleries (Shill & Tonner, 2003). In addition to its other functions, the library has begun to assume a role in the cultural and social life of the institution (Finnerty, 2002; Sannwald, 2001). Interestingly, the only non-library spaces that decreased from the old library to the new were academic departments. This is perhaps an indication of the gradual lessening of emphasis on faculty influence in many new libraries. It is also reflected in the amount of faculty only study space in new libraries, which will be discussed later.

Technology

Not surprisingly, technology infrastructure was improved and expanded in new academic library buildings. Of the 55 respondents that answered the question about wireless network coverage in the new building, only four reported less than 75% coverage in the new building. Eighty percent of respondents (n=44) reported wireless coverage in 100% of the new building, while seven libraries reported wireless coverage in at least three-quarters of the new building. In addition, despite the proliferation of laptops and other portable computing devices, new libraries continue to add more public access computers. None of the responding libraries reported *fewer* public access computers in the new building. Ninety-six percent of the respondents (n=53) reported more public access computers in the new building versus the old facility. Similarly, most libraries reported that increasing the amount of electrical outlets for patron use was an important design consideration for the new facility. While crosstabs revealed a pattern of high numbers of public access computers in the new library with larger floor space, increasing the number of public access computers was distributed across all enrollment profiles and Carnegie classifications. Clustering occurred among libraries reporting 50 to 99 public access computers in the new library (24% of respondents) and 100-149 (18% of respondents) and 200-299 public access computers (18% of respondents). Three respondents indicated more than 400 public access computers in the new library.

Many technology infrastructure issues investigated in prior studies are resolved to a certain degree in academic library buildings completed in the current era. For example, 100% wireless network coverage is available in 80% of the libraries in the current study, while 100% wireless coverage was available in only 24.6% of new libraries completed between 1995 and 2002 (Shill & Tonner, 2003). A number of areas of information technology, however, still deserve comparison, beginning with the new library's investment in public area computing. Despite the proliferation of portable computing devices on college campuses, libraries continue to increase the number of computers available to users. None of the libraries in the current study indicated that there were fewer public area computers in the new space compared with the old facility. Fifty-one percent of the libraries in the current study indicated that there more than 100 public area computers in the new library versus 24% in the Shill and Tonner study. As the "information commons" concept has continued to grow in popularity over the past decade, libraries have converted or combined traditional reference space into multipurpose computing areas offering students access to an array of technologies and technology-related services. Often, the reference function has been integrated into the information commons, with an IT professional staffing the desk alongside a librarian. Larger libraries, most with information commons or areas(s) with similar designations, reported having more computers.

The relationship between an institution's enrollment and the number of computers is fairly straightforward. In general, the higher the institution's enrollment, the greater the number of publicly available computers in the new library building. As computers typically require more table space per person (Boone, 2002), a new library's investment in public area workstations is likely based on a variety of additional factors, including amount of space for collections and quiet study.

Seating

As new libraries have become larger, user space as measured in the amount of library seating available has also increased. Fifty-five respondents answered the three questions in the survey about general-use seating and soft seating. Fifty-three reported an increase in general use seating compared to the old facility. None of the libraries reported a decrease in general use seating in the new facilities compared to the old. Soft seating, typically described as lounges, couches, and other types of non-task specific chairs (e.g., computer table chairs), also increased dramatically in new libraries. Fifty-one libraries responded that there is "significantly more" soft seating available in the new building, while only one library reported that the amount of soft seating had decreased. As expected, the amount of soft seating is significantly correlated with total building project cost ($p<.01$). The amount of library soft seating available in new libraries was also generally greater at residential institutions.

Access and Policy

Another area of inquiry into user space in new libraries concerned access and policy. For the purposes of this survey, access entails user rights to the library spaces, while policy covers the levels at which behavior is regulated in the space. One policy element, quiet study areas, will be discussed in detail in the next chapter. Another is food and beverages. Responses to this survey indicate that the trend of allowing food and beverages in the library space continues apace. Fifty-one libraries provided responses to this question. Of these, approximately 66% (n=37) indicated that food and beverages were allowed in the new space. Other respondents reported allowing food and/or beverages under certain conditions, such as allowing beverages and prohibiting food or allowing only covered beverages. Respondents were also allowed to provide additional information regarding their library's food and beverage policies. These responses illustrate some of the challenges faced by academic libraries as they become more permissive to changing user behavior. While many of these responses offered clarification on the parameters of some food and beverage policies such as prohibiting food and beverages in special collections/archives, many of the other responses show that there is a good deal of ambivalence about these policies among library staff. Adding to ambivalence is an often complex framework for how and where in the facility to enforce the rules, both for the patron and the librarian. For example, one respondent wrote:

> Coffee bar is on first floor; 2nd and 3rd floors are library designated areas. Food/drink allowed in 1st floor; covered beverages elsewhere.

Another wrote:

> Food and beverages permitted in part of the building. Beverages in covered containers allowed except in computer areas.

Other responses provided further examples of policies that, because of the wide range of materials and technology in the library space, are bound to remain confusing as library buildings blend social and academic activity. To the point, another theme that emerged from these written responses centered on the frustration faced by library staff in enforcing these rules. It is worth noting here that these responses came primarily from library deans and directors. One respondent summed up this theme by stating that, "unfortunately, the rule is not enforced so we do find food.... Our main concern is that no damage is done by food & drink in the library."

Increases in the size and the scope of these new libraries could be expected to have an effect on the amount of access provided to the new facilities as well as policies governing behavior in the buildings. As the physical library space serves more purposes and in general becomes more inviting as a social as well as solitary space, it follows that more students would demand to be in the building for more hours. Nearly two-thirds of the libraries in the survey reported increased hours in the new facility, and more than a third of the respondents indicated that 24-hour access was offered to at least part of the facility. The broad majority of libraries offering 24-hour access, however, were on residential campuses. If access to the library facility is used as a measure of value for students (and, given the growing number of academic libraries that offer 24-hour access, it surely is), those on residential campuses enjoy an advantage.

As the library space is liberalized, so too are user policies. Survey results illustrate the continuing trend towards allowing not only greater access to the library buildings, but also relaxed food and beverage policies within the space. While food and beverage policies are not important in and of themselves, allowing food and beverages in the library illustrates the shifting focus away from the library's role as a protective vault for physical volumes towards a more flexible concept of the space. Only two libraries in the survey, presumably archives and/or special collections, indicated that they do not allow food or beverages in at least part of the facility. Loosening of these kinds of rules can be seen as policy expressions of an inevitable, continued (and quickening) transformation of guidelines for what is and is not permissible in the academic library space. As shown in the textual responses to this section of the survey, many librarians find it hard to adjust to this loosening of policies and often find new, more nuanced rules governing behavior in the library difficult to enforce.

Access may also be understood in terms of access to library services. Even with the rapid expansion of technology-based, self-mediated services such as self-checkout and online reference assistance, the majority of libraries that answered the question reported the same or more service points in the new library compared to the old. More than half of the libraries responding (n=49) to the question about service points indicated that the number of service points have increased in the new facility; with another 36.7% reporting that the number of service points had not changed. Only 13% reported a decline in service points in the new facility. Increases as well as decreases in service points distributed fairly evenly across Carnegie class and enrollment profiles, and there were no institutional or project variables that showed significant correlation with number of service points. However, of the six libraries that indicated declines in the number of service points, five were public institutions. Unfortunately, it was beyond the scope of this study to determine the kinds of services (in particular, the balance between traditional and "new" library services) offered at physical locations in these new libraries, or the factors influencing the decisions to include them in the buildings' designs. Access to the facility is also affected, of course, by the scope of activity occurring there, particularly in light of the library's expanding role in various aspects of the institution's academic and cultural life.

Conclusion

Libraries responding to the survey were representative of the total population of libraries that built new libraries and are larger than the buildings they replaced, especially among doctoral/research institutions with large undergraduate populations. The trend towards multiuse is continuing and is indicative of the library's expanding role in campus life. However, the percentage of space in the new building dedicated for library purposes generally increases with the level of undergraduate enrollment. Among the most common non-library facilities being included in new library buildings are general use classrooms and computer labs, cafes, and meeting rooms. The number of library service points in new buildings, while not major planning factors, is not declining. Technological challenges present in older buildings have largely been resolved in new library space and, despite the proliferation of portable computing devices, nearly all libraries in the survey reported significantly more public access computers in the new building. Most libraries also reported less restrictive food and beverage policies in the new space. Finally, library hours are also increasing, and the trend toward 24-hour access is continuing, especially for new libraries on residential campuses. Libraries are being designed around user needs. The next chapter will explore specific aspects of user space in new libraries, particularly learning space.

chapter eight

USER SPACE

Several characteristics of these new buildings reflect the library's changing role in campus life. While fewer libraries were built between 2003-2009, those that were offer more (and more varied) user space. User space can be found along a spectrum of purposes in new library buildings and is not limited to space defined for student use. Libraries are also being increasingly designed to express the expanding role of the library in the social and cultural life of the institution (McDonald, 2002; Rizzo, 2002). Student considerations remain of primary importance, however, especially in terms of various types of learning space. While different types of learning no doubt take place throughout the library, learning spaces for the purposes of this study were defined generally as classroom and study space. Study space includes group studies and other collaborative study areas as well as quiet study. Bennett (2003, 2005) argues for the need to design libraries around learning, as extensions of the classroom. As discussed earlier, in planning new libraries, changing expectations of students for a more comfortable, accessible, and learning-centered library is measurably more important that providing space for physical collections.

Seating

These expectations begin with basics such as plentiful and comfortable library seating. Shill and Tonner's 2003 study found that most libraries are increasing the number of general-use seats, which may include table chairs, computing chairs, and soft seating. As new libraries have become larger, user space as measured in the amount of available seating has also increased. Fifty-five respondents answered the three questions in the survey about general-use seating and soft seating. Less than 10% of new libraries reported fewer than 100 seats and approximately one-third of respondents reported up to 1000 seats in new building. Fifty-three reported an increase in general use seating compared to the old facility. None of the libraries reported a decrease in general use seating in the new facilities compared to the old. Soft seating, typically described as lounges, couches, and other types of non-task specific chairs (e.g., computer table chairs), also increased dramatically in new libraries. Ninety-one percent of survey respondents indicated the addition of more soft seating in the new library: fifty-one libraries responded that there is "significantly more" soft seating available in the new building, while only one library reported that the amount of soft seating had decreased. As expected, the amount of soft seating is significantly correlated with total building project cost ($p<.01$). Campus setting plays a role in the amount of seating in new buildings,

TABLE 30
Number of General Use Seats in New Libraries (n = 58)

	Frequency	Percent	Cumulative Percent
Less than 100	7	12.5	12.5
100–499	19	33.9	46.4
500–999	17	30.4	76.8
1000–1499	8	14.3	91.1
1500–1999	2	3.6	94.6
2000+	3	5.4	100.0
Total	56	96.6	
Missing	2	3.4	
Total	58	100.0	

TABLE 31 Group Study Rooms in New Library Compared to Old Building				
	Frequency	Percent	Valid Percent	Cumulative Percent
Significantly More (50% +)	50	86.2	90.9	90.9
About the Same	3	5.2	5.5	96.4
Fewer	2	3.4	3.6	100.0
Total	55	94.8	100.0	
Missing	3	5.2		
Total	58	100.0		

with libraries on residential campuses offering significantly more seating than libraries on non-residential campuses irrespective of enrollment levels.

Learning Space: Group Study

Libraries are also including significantly more group study in new buildings. The survey asked participants to respond to a series of questions about the number of group study rooms and classrooms included in the new facility. Ninety-one percent of the respondents indicated that their new building included more than 50% more group study space than the old facility. Three libraries indicated that the number of group study rooms remained the same, and only one library reported a decrease in group study space in the new building. Approximately half of the new libraries offer between 11 and 29 group study rooms. The largest number of responses (14) indicated between 20 and

Table 32 Number of Group Study Rooms in New Library Compared to Old Building				
Number of Group Study Rooms	Frequency	Percent	Valid Percent	Cumulative Percent
None	2	3.4	3.5	3.5
1–5	7	12.1	12.3	15.8
6–10	12	20.7	21.1	36.8
11–19	14	24.1	24.6	61.4
20–29	12	20.7	21.1	82.5
30+	10	17.2	17.5	100.0
Total	57	98.3	100.0	
Missing	1	1.7		
Total	58	100.0		

29 group study rooms in the new library. A noticeable number of libraries (10) reported more than 30 group study rooms in the new building. Total enrollment and total square footage is related to the number of group study rooms. Whether an institution is public or private is also related to number of group study rooms in the new library. A cross-tabulation shows that eight of the nine libraries reporting more than 30 group study rooms were at public institutions, while eight of the 13 libraries reporting 20 to 29 group study rooms were at public institutions. There are no significant relationships between institutional enrollment profile, Carnegie classification, or setting and the number of group study rooms at these new libraries.

Shill and Tonner (2003) describe the addition of collaborative/group studies as "an essential component" of modern library design (p. 450). They conclude that not enough group study space is being included in new library facilities. More than half of the respondents in their study indicated between 6 and 15 group studies in the new facility. While the current study can offer no observations on appropriate levels of group study space for new libraries, results do show large percentages of new libraries indicating more than 11 and up to 29 group studies, and a noticeable number of respondents indicating more than 30 group studies in the new facility. Libraries at residential as well as non-residential institutions showed significant increases

TABLE 33
Enrollment Profile and Number of Library Classrooms in New Facility

	Number of Library Classrooms					
	None	1–2	3–5	6–9	10–14	Total
Exclusively Undergraduate	0	4	2	1	1	8
	.0%	50.0%	25.0%	12.5%	12.5%	100.0%
Very High Undergraduate	0	8	5	3	0	16
	.0%	50.0%	31.2%	18.8%	.0%	100.0%
High Undergraduate	1	10	7	1	0	19
	5.6%	52.6%	36.8%	5.3%	.0%	100.0%
Majority Undergraduate	0	7	3	0	0	10
	.0%	70.0%	30.0%	.0%	.0%	100.0%
Majority Graduate/Professional	0	1	0	0	0	1
	.0%	100.0%	.0%	.0%	.0%	100.0%
Exclusively Graduate/ Professional	1	2	0	0	0	3
	33.3%	66.7%	.0%	.0%	.0%	100.0%
Total	2	32	17	5	1	57
	1.9%	57.7%	28.8%	9.6%	1.9%	100.0%

in the amount of group studies in the new facilities, indicating that collaborative study space is important in libraries across institutional categories.

Learning Space: Library Classrooms

More library classrooms are being built into these new facilities, indicating that the new space is meeting a need for either an existing or anticipated expansion of the library's instructional programming. Classrooms designated for library use increased in 84% of the 55 libraries responding to this question in the survey. The number of classrooms remained the same in the remaining 16% of reporting libraries. Fifty-seven libraries indicated a range for the number of library classrooms in the new facility. Thirty-two (56%) of the new libraries offer 1–2 classrooms, and 17 (30%) reported between three and five classrooms. Five libraries reported 6-9 classrooms, one library reported 10–14 new classrooms and no library reported 15 or more classrooms for library use only. A cross-tab analysis reveals that four of the five libraries reporting a range of 10 to 14 library-only classrooms are at institutions with either exclusive or very high undergraduate student populations.

The fact that most new facilities included library classrooms may indicate the growing role the library has in teaching information literacy skills across the curriculum, in par-

TABLE 34
Amount of Space Designated for Quiet Study in New Library Compared to Old Library

Enrollment Profile	More	About the Same	Less	No Quiet Study Space	Total
Exclusive Undergraduate	2	1	3	2	8
	25.0%	12.5%	37.5%	25.0%	100.0%
Very High Undergraduate	8	3	1	3	15
	53.3%	20.0%	6.7%	20.0%	100.0%
High Undergraduate	13	3	0	2	18
	72.2%	10.0%	.0%	11.1%	100.0%
Majority Undergraduate	7	1	0	2	10
	70.0%	10%	.0%	20.0%	100.0%
Majority Graduate Professional	0	1	0	0	1
	.0%	100.0%	.0%	.0%	100.0%
Exclusive Graduate Professional	0	2	1	0	3
	.0%	50.0%	50.0%	.0%	100.0%
Total	30	11	5	9	55
	54.5%	20.0%	9.1%	16.4%	100.0%

ticular the undergraduate curriculum. A general pattern that emerges from the results is that of more classroom space in libraries at institutions with higher undergraduate populations. Classroom space can be costly (especially if it is not used), and the number of classrooms may be seen as an indicator of the library's level of engagement in student learning. Lombardi and Wall (2005) describe the library's (specifically, the recent library building and addition at Duke University) role in learning as that of a "gateway" rather than a "gatekeeper" (p. 17.2). In general, the library will assume an expanding role in the curriculum in coming years (Freeman, 2005; King, 2000). No doubt the inclusion of added classroom space in new libraries is in part the result of the growing importance of information literacy, which has begun to translate into institutional support for library-led information literacy programming (such as the highly successful program at Purdue University) across much of the undergraduate program.

Learning Space: Quiet Study

Quiet study was an important feature of new library space for a majority of the respondents. Fifty-five percent (n=30) reported that there is more space designated for quiet study in the new space versus the old. Twenty percent (n=11) reported that the amount of space designated for quiet study had remained the same in the new building. Fourteen libraries, however, indicated that there was either less or no space designated for quiet study in the new building. Nonetheless, one of the more traditional functions of the library space, quiet study, is an important consideration in library design. Peterson (2005) describes the vital "culture of silence" that users ascribe to the library space (p. 63). Others have outlined the role quiet study space plays in the library's support of student learning (Demas, 2005; Ranseen, 2002) and the vital connection between solitary study and discovery (Crawford, 1999). While approximately 20% of the libraries in the study reported that the amount of quiet study in the new library remained the same as the old building, 50% indicated an increase in the amount of quiet study space. Study results show that more quiet study space is most common at institutions with 75% to 90% undergraduate enrollments. Interestingly, however, more than half of the institutions with exclusively undergraduate populations reported less or no areas in the new facility designated for quiet study (see Table 34).

Faculty Space

Faculty and graduate student space has long been an important consideration in library design. Faculty carrels, for example, have been part of life at college and university libraries for decades, especially research libraries. This survey sought to assess the importance of faculty space as an element in the design of new library buildings. Participants were asked to compare the number of faculty carrels in the old facility to the new. Fifty of the 53 libraries in the study responded to this question. While some libraries responded that there were no faculty carrels in the old building, far more responded that there were no faculty carrels in the new facility. This analysis, however, focused on whether a facility includes faculty carrels in the new space. While 25% of respondents indicated that faculty carrel space had increased in the new building, libraries that did not include faculty carrels exceeded those that included carrels by a ratio that approached 3:1. Half of the respondents (n=28) reported that there were no faculty carrels in the old facility, while over two thirds, 67% (n=37), reported that there were no faculty carrels in the new facility. Cross-tabulated with Carnegie classifications, approximately 70% of the masters colleges and universities in the survey reported no faculty carrels in the new library space. More than nearly two thirds of doctoral research universities in the survey sample indicated that they did not include faculty carrels the new library building.

As the results indicate, the majority of libraries in the survey did not include specially designated faculty space in the new building. As discussed, this decrease in faculty space was not limited to undergraduate institutions: 70% of the responding libraries at master's colleges and universities and two thirds of the doctoral/research institutions indicated that there were no designated faculty study spaces in the new facility. Antell and Engel's 2004 study at the University of Oklahoma showed that, while use of print resources decreases with "faculty age" (the age of the scholar when he or she received his last degree), younger faculty also showed support for the library space as being conducive for scholarship. While scholars may report that they value the physical library space, digitization of journals, especially in fields such as medicine, engineering, law, and science, makes them less likely to need use of the physical library space. When it comes to planning and input on new library space, faculty typically find a place at the table if they desire one. Decreasing amounts of space for faculty study in these new facilities may indicate diminishing claims on the library space on behalf of the faculty.

While faculty space declined, the amount of space for library staff increased in most of these new libraries. While growth in library staff areas and increasing service did not prove to be major planning factors for new libraries in this study, staff space did increase measurably. It was not clear, however, how this expansion of staff space was allotted along professional and paraprofessional functions, or to what extent that is an indicator of expanding staff levels or simply cramped quarters in the old facility. No matter what these results imply, however, they seem to indicate that the importance of library staff is not compromised in the design of these new buildings. Eighty-eight percent (n=48) of libraries that responded to the question about library staff areas indicated that the amount of space for staff has increased in the new library space. Eleven percent reported decreases in staff space, and only one library responded that space for staff had remained the same. Libraries that showed increases in staff space distributed fairly evenly across Carnegie class and enrollment profiles. Four of the six libraries that lost staff space were public institutions. There were no institutional or project variables that showed significant relationships with the amount of staff space in new libraries.

Conclusion

New library design reflects the importance of providing an expanded, comfortable environment for users, but also the library's evolving role as a learning space. The amount of task and soft seating increased markedly in new library buildings, with even more significant increases in soft seating at residential campus libraries. Group study space is also proliferating in new library buildings, with the largest number of group study rooms reported in libraries at large, public institutions across both residential and non-residential campus settings. As the library's instructional programming expands, more classrooms are also being included in new library buildings, with the largest increases at institutions with large undergraduate student populations. Traditional learning space also remains important, with most libraries in the survey reporting more areas designated for quiet study in the new building. Faculty space, however, appears to be declining across all institutional categories (including doctoral/research universities), with most libraries in the survey reporting less space designated for faculty use in the new facility compared to the old. Library staff space, however, is increasing in most new buildings. Now that planning factors and general characteristics of these new libraries have been described, the next chapter will wrap up the discussion of survey results by providing an overview of how use of these new buildings may be used as measurement of their success.

chapter nine

USAGE

Role of New Library Building in the Academic Life of the Institution

Given the increasing inclusion of learning spaces in new academic libraries, it may be assumed that that library's role in the academic life of the institution is expanding. Other types of spaces in new library buildings represent what could be considered expressions of the library's expanding role in the social and cultural life of the institution (McDonald, 2002; Rizzo, 2002). Survey participants were given the opportunity to, in their own words, list three spaces in their new buildings that best represent the library's role in the academic life of the institution, as well as three spaces that best represent the library's role in the social and cultural life of the institution. Respondents provided a wealth of information, with 163 responses to the first question and 145 responses to the second question. Themes were derived from these responses, and each response was then indexed and coded according to theme. Following that process, the responses were scored according to frequency/theme.

Table 35 lists themes and accompanying scores to the question about space in the new building that best represents the library's role in the academic life of the university. The most common response was classrooms used primarily for library purposes. Most respondents described these spaces with common terms such as "library classroom," while others used terms such as "library instruction labs." Several respondents described the library's role in teaching information literacy with classroom space. "Group and collaborative study space" was listed by 25 respondents. Most respondents described these spaces in simple terms such as "group study" and "collaborative" study spaces. The third most frequently listed space (17 responses) was the

TABLE 35
Spaces in New Building Identified by Respondents as Best Representing the Library's Role in Academic Life of the Institution

Theme	Responses
Library classrooms and instruction labs	37
Group study/collaborative space	26
Information commons/learning commons	19
Reference area/information desk	10
Study space	9
Library collections (stacks, compact shelving, ASRS)	9
Rare books/Archives/Special Collections	9
Reading room	7
Faculty development center	6
Digital media production center	3
24/7 areas	3
Designated space for faculty and/or graduate students	5
Writing and/or tutoring center	3
IT help desk	2
Undergraduate Research Center	1
Soft seating areas	1
Computer workstations	1
Atrium	1

information commons. Respondents described these spaces in a variety of ways. While "information commons" was the most commonly used term, "learning commons" was also used. Many librarians consider the modern reference area to serve several of the same functions as the information commons. Respondents listed reference areas and information desks eight times. Some other interesting areas identified as best representing the library's role in academic life included faculty teaching development centers (six responses); areas designated for faculty and/or graduate student work only; and space and functions related to the collection, including compact shelving, open stacks, and automatic storage retrieval systems.

Interestingly, there is nothing that could necessarily be considered exclusive to the library in group studies and classrooms. These spaces, while they truly add value to the library, are not unique to the library in the way that book stacks, reading rooms, and reference desks are unique (and have, for centuries, visually and functionally defined the library's physical space) to the library. These more traditional spaces, however, were identified only a handful of times in comparison to library classrooms, group studies, and information commons. In summary, in response to the question regarding areas of the new building that best represented the library's academic role in the institution, respondents most frequently listed learning, instructional, and collaborative spaces.

Role of New Library Building in the Social/Cultural Life of the Institution

With a few exceptions, spaces identified as representing the library's evolving role in the social and cultural life of the institution were markedly different from those identified as representing the library's academic role, but they were no less varied. There was a wide difference between the most frequently listed themes and the remaining spaces. As with the first question, some responses were eliminated and therefore not included in themes due to the ambiguity of the response (e.g., "second level"). The area that was represented most frequently as representing the new building's role in the social and cultural life of the institution was the coffee bar/café (22 responses). The areas mentioned with the next greatest frequency were meeting rooms.

Meeting and conference rooms in new libraries were described as having many purposes and varying in size and grandeur, from community meeting space to the newly designated location for a university's board of trustee meetings. The third most commonly identified spaces fall under the category of art gallery, display, and exhibit space. These include a variety of areas in these new buildings where artwork is hung (one library reported having 1500 linear feet of hanging space) and various exhibits are presented. A sampling of other responses to this question includes reading rooms (nine responses), lounges, and, interestingly, atriums and other areas closely linked to outdoors (five responses). Respondents generally used more descriptive, laudatory language to describe areas in the new building that they considered important to the social and cultural life at the institution. For example, one respondent reported that the new library is "known as the place to be," while others described spaces as "beautiful" and "well designed."

A few spaces made both the academic and social/cultural lists. One such space was the reading room. Grand reading rooms are enjoying resurgence in academic library design, often a consequence of an institution's broader strategy to have the new library serve as a functional as well as symbolic showpiece of institutional pride (Hickey, 2001). Reading rooms and other iconic spaces in modern libraries are also a visually effective way of illustrating the library's role in integrating the past and future (Michalek, 2004). Still, it is interesting to note that the reading room was identified more times as representing the library's

TABLE 36 Spaces in New Building Identified by Respondents as Best Representing the Library's Role in the Social and Cultural Life of the Institution	
Theme	Responses
Café/coffee bar	25
Meeting rooms	16
Art gallery, display, and exhibit space	17
Reading room	12
Computer labs	11
General seating (including soft seating)	6
24-hour study areas	2
Atrium and outdoor space	5
Group study rooms	7
Auditorium	3
Information commons	3
Archives/Special Collections	8
Multiuse, unfurnished areas	8
Public area computers	1
Media production room	1
Lounges	2
New book area	2
Study areas	3
Leisure/popular reading collection	1
Faculty development center	1
Public corridor	2

role in the cultural and social life of the institution than it was identified as having a role in the academic life of the institution.

What Fisher (2005) terms the "drama of community" (which draws users to the physical library) was expressed through some of the additional comments in this section of the survey. These comments also served to clarify specific uses of some of the social and academic spaces listed by the respondents. The difference between activity in library meeting rooms and collaborative study spaces was distinct. For example, community groups and university trustees use meeting rooms while students primarily use group studies. In general, there was notable enthusiasm expressed by many respondents in describing the role these academic and social/cultural spaces play in the success of their new libraries.

Use of the Building

The last section of the survey focused on use of the new library building. Respondents were asked to describe usage levels in terms of percentages of use increases or declines. Respondents were also asked to project building use for the next year and compare it to gate count data from the current year. Percentage ranges rather than whole numbers were used for the sake of response expediency and because it was anticipated that most respondents would not be able to easily acquire gate data across multiple years. This assumption proved true given the low number of responses when respondents were given the opportunity (optional) to provide exact gate counts for the last full, pre-construction years in the old facility and the latest full year in the new facility. Respondents were also asked to list the three busiest areas of the facility and were given the opportunity to identify, in their own words, what they consider important measures of facility usage. One of the research questions of this study was to identify relationships between specific building characteristics and post project use.

An overwhelming majority of respondents reported significant increases in building usage compared to the old facility. While not all of the participants answered this question (48 out of the 58 libraries responded), 91.7% (44 libraries) of those that did indicated that use of the new building increased between 25% and 100% over the old building. 8.3% of respondents (4 libraries) reported that use of the new facility increased between 10% and 24% over the old facility. *None* of the respondents indicated that use of the new building had increased only marginally, remained the same, or decreased in comparison to the old facility.

Forty-three libraries answered the question regarding anticipated use of the new building next year compared to the latest year's gate count. Nearly two thirds of the respondents to this question (n=47) indicated that they expected gate counts to remain about the same as the prior year (15 libraries) or increase modestly between one and ten percent (14 libraries). Six libraries indicated that they expected use to increase between 10% and 25%, and 12 libraries indicated that they expected use to increase more than 25% over the latest year. *None* of the libraries anticipated use of the new building to decline in the coming year.

Data collected on use of these new libraries, while not as numerically specific as earlier studies, provides basic information on overall building use in the form of percentage increases or decreases in gate counts. The current study also allowed respondents to identify specific areas of the new building that were among the busiest. Forty-eight libraries provided information on pre- and post-project use. All of these libraries reported increased use of the new facility based on the gate counts from the last full year in the old facility and the latest full year in the new building. Ninety-two percent of the responding libraries (representing over three fourths of all of the libraries in the study) reported usage increases of more than 25%, and none indicated that they anticipated usage to decrease in the coming year. It is clear that, using the common metric of gate counts, these new libraries are successful buildings. With most reporting libraries indicating similar levels of increased usage, it was difficult to determine relationships between specific building features and usage. Due to the uneven response rate to questions about building usage, the scaled nature of response data, and the fact that all responding libraries reported increased current and anticipated usage, it was determined that attempting to link specific building features with usage may not prove fruitful.

Cross-tabs, however, reveal a general pattern of higher use with expanded hours to the facility and availability of wireless networking throughout the building. For libraries that reported heavy increases (more than 25%) in use, increased building usage was most commonly linked with increased hours in the new building versus the old and wireless network coverage. This pattern, however, does not tell the complete story of why these new libraries, even the less-than-new libraries such as those completed in the earlier years covered in this study (e.g., 2003), are so heavily used. For libraries completed in these earlier years, one can assume that the "wow" factor and novelty of a new library has subsided. Yet even these libraries continue to thrive.

For a clearer picture as to why these new buildings are so successful, it was decided that more meaningful explanations could be derived from what the respondents themselves considered to be the busiest areas of the new building. In addition, a follow-up question asking respondents to report unanticipated aspects of usage also proved meaningful in describing why and how these new buildings are so successful. As with previous questions in which respondents were asked to provide written responses, the data were coded according to topic/theme. Fifty-three libraries provided responses to this question. Respondents' written answers provided a wealth of information on how these buildings are being used. While there is

TABLE 37 **Busiest Areas in New Library as Identified by Survey Respondents**	
Theme	Responses
Group study rooms	31
Study areas (includes study tables, carrels, study floors, quiet study)	28
Public area computers	18
Information Commons/Learning Commons	16
Computer labs	10
Café	9
Reading room(s)	1
Classrooms	5
Meeting/conference rooms	4
Soft seating	4
Media Center	3
Lounge	2
Circulation	2
24 hour study area	2
Photocopier	3
Tutoring Center	1
Open areas	1
Reference desk	1
Reference area	2
Information desk	1
Music and media collection/language learning center	1

always a risk posed by respondent subjectivity when collecting data like these, the proximity and familiarity of the reporter to the observation offers advantages over purely numerical data. Indeed, these responses are likely part of the narrative these library leaders use to describe these buildings.

Group study rooms as well as other study spaces were identified as the busiest areas in the libraries. Group study rooms were listed, somewhat specifically, by 31 respondents. Other learning spaces such as classrooms and information commons were also frequently identified as among the busiest spaces in these new buildings. These were the same three spaces that were identified by respondents as best representing the library's role in the academic life of the institution. A far smaller number of responses listed the library's busiest areas that also appeared on the list of the library's social and cultural spaces. Despite multiuse and the expanding role of the library in many aspects of campus life, space that the respondents consider academic in nature and supporting student learning are the busiest in the new library. While not comparable from a numeric standpoint, these results are generally consistent with Shill and Tonner's (2003) findings that the quality of library instruction labs has a very high correlation with post project use, and that the inclusion of social spaces such as coffeehouse has a less pronounced relationship with post-project use.

Other types of study areas that are geared toward individual study were identified with nearly the same frequency as group study areas. The most commonly identified spaces in this category were open study spaces, tables, carrels, study floors, and quiet study areas. Public computing areas came next in terms of frequency of responses, followed by information commons and learning commons and computer labs. Table 37 lists the responses by frequency. By far, however, the library's function of providing study space is the most utilized in new facilities. With the addition of so much collaborative study space in new libraries, however, it is clear that this function is evolving to meet changing student learning behaviors.

In order to discover other means by which libraries measure use of the new facility, this survey also asked respondents to list the three most important measures of facility usage in order of importance. There were 52 responses to this question. Responses clearly indicated that gate counts are considered the most important and most widely used measure of usage. Gate counts were listed most frequently in both the first (24 responses) and second order of importance. Use of the collection as measured through circulation was listed in third order of importance. Among the most commonly listed usage measurements following gate counts were reference questions, technology use, and head counts. A handful of respondents indicated the number of library classes taught as a measure of library use. Interestingly, several respondents also identified use of online resources as an important measure of facility use.

Finally, respondents were given the opportunity to report on any aspect of building use that was unexpected. Two-thirds of the survey participants commented on this question. These responses offer an interesting if varied glimpse into how new space is being used—and not used. Several themes emerge from the responses. One of the more common observations was the popularity and demand for the new building as a marquee space for academic, administrative, social, and cultural events that most likely would have not taken place in the old facility. Several respondents seemed surprised by this even given the fact that the new library was, as one respondent pointed out, planned for such purposes. Another respondent added that the meeting and exhibit space was "booked all the time with community as well as academic events." As another respondent put it, "any high-profile event takes place here." At least two libraries reported that unanticipated demand resulted in competition and friction between academic departments for library classroom space. One respondent, presumably from a science library, reported being pleasantly surprised by large number of social science and humanities students making use of the new facility.

Respondents provided mixed observations on the way some traditional library space and services were being used in the new building. Two libraries reported a dramatic drop in reference transactions, while a handful of other libraries reported a surprising surge in the use of print collections after the new library opened. One library reported an unexpected rise in faculty demand for more carrels, while another library reported that use of faculty and graduate student study carrels was so low they were given over to general student use to meet undergraduate demand Another respondent expressed disappointment in the lack of use of the study carrels installed in the new building. As for the proliferation of social and collaborative space alongside traditional study spaces, at least one respondent was surprised that "students really do want it to be quiet!" Perhaps highlighting the difference between undergraduate, collaborative study and individually focused graduate study, one library director reported that graduate students spend more time in large, open study areas than in student lounges. Several libraries reported unanticipated interest and use in the new library by the neighboring community. Finally, several respondents pointed out that they did not expect the students to, as one respondent put it, "make the space their own" with such ease and directness, as exemplified by student use of the new library for a variety of purposes beyond research and study.

Conclusion

New academic library buildings are heavily used, even years after opening. Most of the buildings in the survey reported significant increases in use of the new facility when compared to the old, and none expected declines in use in the coming years. As libraries incorporate more learning space, classrooms and collaborative studies were reported by respondents as best representing the library's evolving role in the academic life of the institution. These new libraries also play a role in the social and cultural life of the institution as illustrated by the popularity of cafes, art galleries, and meeting space that are often included in the new building. The busiest areas of these new libraries are typically linked to the library's academic function, namely group studies, followed by more traditional spaces such as quiet study. While the library's role as a learning space is paramount, the popularity of these new buildings extends beyond the academic function. Success is also measured by the popularity of these new buildings as centers of institutional life.

chapter ten

CONCLUSION

The current era has been one of unprecedented transformation for academic libraries. One could argue that libraries have undergone more change in the past 20 years than in the past two centuries (Dillon, 2008). During that time, the debate over the future of the library building has moved from dire predictions of building obsolescence in the wake of digitization to, in recent years, the re-emergence of the library as a center of campus life. While there are fewer new academic libraries being built, those that have been completed are generally larger, busier, and grander than the buildings they replaced. Many are popular campus destinations. What happens inside those buildings can tell us much about how librarianship is evolving and, to a certain degree, point to new intersections for the library with various aspects of the parent institution's values and mission. Certainly, the design and use of new library space can tell us how far we have come in meeting the challenges and opportunities that continue to transform the role the library in the academic enterprise.

Background

Over the past several years, research on academic library planning and design has explored a variety of factors shaping new library space. Increasingly informed by new frameworks in educational architecture, the expansion of learning space in new libraries is the subject of ongoing research and inquiry. In general, literature on new academic library projects provides witness to the expanding role the library is playing in student education, particularly undergraduate education. The coming years will tell how successful new library design has been in providing the types of space that make this possible. Another area of inquiry in recent years has been the ever-changing balance between the library space and physical collections. There are few more visible expressions of the rapid change underway in our profession than the library's physical space. Interestingly, debate over library design often leads to more critical conversations surrounding the enduring importance of the printed book in education, research, and scholarly communication. The monograph aside, digitization continues to change the way scholars research and students learn across a wide range of disciplines. Evidence of the implications of digitization for the library space is often profound, particularly for libraries that serve disciplines in which the migration of scholarly material to digital formats has been swiftest. Finally, as the primacy of print collections as focal point of library space gradually wanes, research and building project descriptions provide numerous examples in recent years of user-centered design, multiuse facilities, and, overall, highly successful new buildings.

This study would not have taken shape without the thoughtful and thorough previous studies on library buildings conducted around the beginning of this century. I am very grateful to those whose work provided me with a starting point for my own exploration. The survey used in this study was an amalgamation of previous instruments as well as new avenues of exploration. Like any survey, this one was far from perfect. Future researchers may find the design useful, however, as I found surveys used in previous studies helpful in designing the instrument for this study. I am very grateful to previous researchers as well as my many colleagues who offered their feedback during the pilot phase of this study. The survey is their work as well as mine.

In many ways, this study continues the ongoing efforts in the profession to inventory, measure, and evaluate new library space during a time of great transformation for academic libraries in general. At the very least, it explores what one could consider to be a number of major elements involved in planning, design, and use of new library space. By limiting itself to new construction only, however, this study focused on a specific aspect of the evolution of the academic library. There is perhaps no more revealing measure of an institution's commitment to the role of the library in the enterprise of higher education than the construction of a new library building.

Overview of New Academic Library Construction

Because there is so much information available about new library projects, it is appropriate to provide an overview of academic library building activity before one gets to the specifics of planning and design, which are better addressed using a survey. This pre-survey overview provides useful data on many levels, and answers the general question of whether library construction is increasing or declining in the current era. When measured against the seven years prior to the current study, construction of new academic library buildings has declined sharply. Public institutions, typically with larger enrollments, built larger, more expensive libraries at a lower cost lower cost per student and, not surprisingly, offer significantly less square footage per student than their private university counterparts. In current library design, particular attention is being paid to undergraduate student populations. While library construction is down overall, construction of new libraries at predominately undergraduate institutions has actually increased when compared to the seven years prior to this study. In addition, more money is spent per student on library space at institutions with larger undergraduate enrollments. It would appear that new library space is being geared heavily towards undergraduate populations. A general (if often misapplied) rule of academic librarianship is that undergraduate students use the library for space and services, while faculty and graduate students use the library for collections. If this is true, then we may be seeing a precipitous decline in the value our faculty in many (but certainly not all) disciplines place in the library as a physical place. This disconnectedness from the library space presents several challenges for librarians who will need to work hard to keep faculty aware of the continued importance of the library's physical space as research collections and other staples of faculty and graduate level scholarship migrate to digital formats. Of course, there are many compelling stories to share with faculty, especially the library's evolving role as a learning space and a powerful center and symbol of the undergraduate academic experience. Still, space dedicated exclusively for faculty use is declining in new library buildings, indicating that faculty were either not at the table during the planning process (unlikely) or simply do not see a need for amenities such as faculty study carrels when so much of what they need for their work is available online. What is most crucial is to ensure that, while faculty may not use the library physical space in ways they once did, they are still supportive of the library's efforts to preserve and enhance the space for existing (and, often, still expanding) physical collections, education, and campus academic and cultural life.

Investigating New Academic Library Space

After identifying overall construction activity and general patterns, this study sought to next answer deeper questions about how new academic libraries are planned, designed, and, ultimately, used. Several interesting themes emerged first from inquiries into planning factors for new libraries. As the risk of turning a library pun, a very surprising finding of this study is the relatively short shelf life of many of the library buildings being replaced by new facilities. On college and university campuses where classroom and administrative buildings often date to the 19th century, replacing library buildings that are between 25 and 49 years old seems incongruous. While we should not judge our colleagues from the 1960s through the 1980s for failing to plan for a digital revolution that would come with such intensity and speed, the rapid obsolescence of these buildings illustrates the risks associated with planning facilities around a single function. In the case of library buildings for the better part of the 20th Century, this function was primarily a place for storage and access for an ever-expanding amount of printed material.

What we can see now is that we are adapting, even thriving, in the way we devise new library space around student needs and learning rather than exclusively print collections. Indeed, the way new libraries are being planned reveals a good deal about how we view the primacy of printed material in the library of the future. With nearly two thirds of the libraries in this study reporting either stagnant or declining levels of print acquisitions, it is clear that the visual identity of the library will continue to push away from the long reigning iconography of book stacks. This is not to say that the monograph will disappear from the library space, of course, merely that it has begun to share the space with other elements of the library building, including classrooms, new types of study space, cultural and social space, meeting rooms, art galleries, and more. No one element will be dominant. As shown in this study as well as numerous other examples of library renovation and projects around the country, this new model for library space has already begun to emerge. Modern library planning and design has become a nuanced process in which the changing role of the academic library is articulated through the design of spaces serving multiple purposes that, while seemingly disparate, reflect long held library values of creating scholarly community, providing access to information, and teaching skills necessary to transform information into knowledge.

Perhaps the most visible sign of this transformation of the library space is the inclusion of such a large amount of learning space in new library buildings. While some could argue that the library has always been a learning space, the types of spaces in new libraries diverge greatly from the tables and book stacks of yesterday. New libraries are including more classrooms, collaborative space such as group studies, while also more traditional, individual learning space such as carrels and "quiet study" areas throughout the new building. Learning space in new libraries expands in proportion to the level of undergraduate student enrollment. While some caution that we should not equate success with getting "bodies to a room" (Dillon, 2008, p. 52), the proliferation of learning space in new libraries is a result not only of planning for this role, but also the waning of print collections as a primary consumer of library square footage (particularly, free standing and bound journals.). During the planning and design process, learning space can be reclaimed from floor space that would have been earmarked for print collections less than a generation ago. As will be discussed shortly, current and future research will be useful in assessing these learning spaces and, indeed, if modern academic libraries have become, as some cynics would argue, mere high-tech study halls. While I doubt this is true, it will be interesting to learn more about the type of learning taking place in these new spaces and the strength of the relationship to the library's mission and purpose. For example, is the library evolving to become as much a classroom building as a center for research and information access? Clearly, as is shown though survey data, these new buildings being increasingly designed for multiuse as the library begins to incorporate many elements of what would once only have been more typically found in traditional academic buildings, administration centers, and student centers.

Multiuse includes non-library classrooms and computer labs, but also many other elements not found in legacy library buildings where large amounts of space have been given over to book stacks as collections have grown over the years. The success of these new buildings as measured by gate counts is undeniable. Art galleries, auditoriums, and meeting space are among the most common manifestations of multiuse, as are non-library classroom and computer labs. While the library is an obvious manifestation of the institution's academic function, it is also clear that new library buildings often offer even more, and are increasingly centers for social and cultural activity as well. Many respondents provided testimony to the new library building as marquee place on campus, one that is often used for high profile events outside of the academic function. It is hard not to argue that this is a positive trend. Future planners and designers of library space can take notice that stakeholders throughout the institution will expect new library buildings to represent and serve a variety of aspects of institutional life. A decade ago, when there was a high level of anxiety about the future of the library building, it would have been hard to imagine the vibrancy and success evidenced by so many of the facilities completed since 2003. Multiuse enables the library to serve as a center for a variety of aspects of campus life while, hopefully, strengthening the library's core academic mission.

Further Research

By using certain basic descriptors such as public/private governance, size and setting, and enrollment profile, it was possible to outline new library construction using a framework that may be useful for further research. Similarly, while the process of identifying new library projects for inclusion in this study was extensive, the methodology will hopefully be of use to future researchers and others who are interested in U.S. academic library construction. Cost, size, and many other useful data on new library space are readily available from a variety of sources. That said, while there are some major annual sources of information about library construction, these sources are by no means exhaustive. A national database of library building projects would be extremely helpful. The inventory of projects completed between 2003 and 2009 created for this study may provide a foundation on which to build.

By using a quantitative method, this study aimed to garner a significant amount of general and specific knowledge that extends previous research and fills a gap in the data on new academic library buildings completed in the first decade of this new century. This study adds to the body of knowledge by comparing data with previous research and identifying emerging and continuing trends based on these comparisons. This approach, however, does not speak to the specific stories about what is happening in new academic library spaces, nor does it explore user perspectives beyond the observations of the librarians answering the survey. The quantitative approach limits itself primarily to specifically measurable data. Qualitative methods, on the other hand, offer opportunities for detailed analysis and detail (Patton, 2002). This study provided several opportunities for participants to offer responses to questions in their own words, and many of these responses yielded useful information that was used primarily to augment the quantitative analysis. These written responses and the accompanying analysis of these responses, however, should not be construed as inductive qualitative inquiry. Research on the changing physical academic library space should certainly be conducted using qualitative methods such as case studies, focus groups, and in-depth interviews with library planners, practitioners, and, most importantly, library users. Qualitative inquiry would be highly appropriate for follow-up work to this quantitative study.

Several themes emerging from both parts of this study invite further quantitative as well as qualitative inquiry. While the study of the population revealed a general downward trend in academic library construction, it did not explore library renovations and smaller additions, nor library construction at community colleges, as have previous studies. The current study could be extended and enhanced by including these types of projects, which would provide a more complete, quantitative analysis of the level of investment being made in academic libraries in the current era. Further study could also investigate the balance in new library construction among different types of libraries on multi-library campuses to identify factors affecting closures, expansions, and consolidations of branch and departmental libraries. The downward emphasis on faculty space in new libraries can also be explored further to determine if declining levels of dedicated faculty studies, as shown in this study, signifies a broader trend of faculty disengagement with the physical library, or is the result of faculty making use of the library space in new ways. It may also be useful to investigate how library operating budgets are affected when a new building is completed, including an analysis of how changes in the physical library operating space affect allocations for new staff and service activity occurring in that space.

Investigating the effect of declining funding for public colleges and universities on library construction in the coming years could also prove useful for library planners. To this point, further inquiry into the differences between library construction spending (on a per student basis) at public versus private institutions may reveal further differences in planning, design, and use of libraries between the two types of institutions, especially if the analysis extends to public universities beyond large flagship campuses. In addition, with so much learning space being built into these new facilities, it may be useful to explore possible relationships between amount and quality of instruction space and depth of the library's information literacy programming, as well as library instruction across the undergraduate curriculum in general. Also, as more students use learning spaces and other elements of the new physical library facility, there are opportunities for research into how students measure the value of the library space: not specifically, as there are already library quality assessment instruments for this, but compared to other campus facilities with similar types of spaces. Finally, as many libraries further reduce acquisition of print-based material, continued research into how libraries devise for and utilize bookless spaces in new as well as existing spaces should be highly useful for library planners and practitioners alike.

Concluding Note

As higher education's expectations for academic libraries change, new library buildings are both extensions of institutional function and expressions of institutional values. At most colleges and universities, there is tremendous pressure to distribute physical and financial resources as effectively as possible given growing constraints on institutional budgets and increased calls for efficiency and accountability by a range of external as well as internal constituents. As an institution begins to consider building a new library facility, it is important for library planners to have an understanding of the level of investment similar institutions have made in new library space, as well as the return on that investment in terms of building functionality and use. Data from this study should provide decision-makers with useful information on academic library building projects in the current era in general, but also the relationship between institutional variables such as governance, setting, and enrollment and the size and cost of new libraries at institutions across similar categories.

This study provides library planners and practitioners with information on how new library buildings are being designed and, more importantly, how they are being used. Data from libraries in this study illustrate how new attributes and functions of these spaces add value to library and institutional mission. As reflected through new library design, for example, the library's role has expanded beyond provision, access, and organization of information to include a more active role in student learning. An important illustration of evolving library mission as reflected through new library design is the success of library building projects in meeting the growing need in higher education to provide learning space beyond the traditional classroom. Equally important, as institutions build more (and more varied) learning space into new library buildings, learning agendas specific to the library, such as teaching information literacy, are served as well.

Data from this study also provides library planners with information on a range of additional purposes for which new academic libraries are being designed, as well as how library leaders gauge the success of these new spaces for these purposes. Many of these design elements, such as expanding technology infrastructure and adding more quiet as well as group study space, are familiar themes that should be considered essential hallmarks of good library design. Other themes such as a growing presence of social and collaborative space and the expansion of the library's role as a cultural, organizational, and social center of campus life should be of great interest to library planners and practitioners alike. Academic library buildings are evolving rapidly in the current era. The library's physical identity, long dominated by the book, has incorporated numerous new elements in recent years, and is likely to assume more in the coming years.

As planning considerations for academic libraries change and uses for the physical space become more varied, the library's purpose in the higher education enterprise is enhanced and extended. Data from this study provides library planners, practitioners, and other interested parties with empirical data on planning factors, usage, space characteristics, and other design elements to support decision-making as they consider new academic library buildings, or equally important, evaluate how existing space is used. While digitization and networked information will continue to change the way the library approaches its more traditional roles of acquisition, access, and preservation of collections, it is clear from the success of library projects in this study that the academic library building has a very important if evolving role to play in higher education. The question need not be if the academic library building will survive in the digital age, but, rather, how it is adapting to thrive in the digital age.

appendix a

SURVEY OF NEW ACADEMIC LIBRARY BUILDINGS 2003–2009

Introduction

Thank you for participating in this study of new academic library building projects completed between 2003 and 2009. This survey contains 53 questions and is divided into six sections. When you have finished each page, click "Continue" to proceed.

Depending on your level of knowledge about the current and former facilities, some questions may require you to locate data. Should you want to scan the survey first, you may exit and re-enter this survey at any time prior to completion provided you are using the same computer and web browser. It is estimated that it will take approximately 30 minutes to complete this survey.

Additional Information for Participants

1. This study requires participants to complete a survey that will require some estimation of data about the library building. It is estimated that the survey will take approximately 30 minutes to complete. This study includes no experimental procedures.

2. This study presents minimal risks for participants. Risks of discomfort are minimal, although respondents may feel that they need more time to complete the survey.

3. By identifying trends in modern library design and usage, library practitioners, university administrators, faculty, and students may use the results of this study to better understand the evolving form and function of the academic library in institutional life. Results of this study may be particularly useful to planners and others involved in academic library building projects. Results of this study will be published in the professional literature and disseminated broadly.

4. Your participation in this study is voluntary. Your confidentiality will be maintained throughout this study and your name will not be published in the results of this survey, nor will the name of your institution. Refusal to participate in this study will involve no penalty or loss. Participants may also discontinue participation at any time.

5. Participants understand that Illinois Institute of Technology is not responsible for any injuries or medical conditions they may suffer during the time they are research subjects unless those injuries or medical conditions are due to IIT's negligence.

6. Participants may direct any questions about this study and their rights as participants to Dr. Christopher Stewart, Dean of Libraries and Principal Investigator (stewart@iit.edu, 312-567-3293) or the Executive Officer of the IIT Institutional Review Board (312-567-7141).

Institutional and Project Data

Please provide institution and project data in this section. After the survey is submitted, additional institutional data derived from Carnegie classifications and the National Center for Educational Statistics will be added by researchers.

Survey of New Academic Library Buildings 2003-2009

1. Institution Name

2. Library Name

3. Person completing survey

4. Title of person completing survey

Survey of New Academic Library Buildings 2003-2009

5. Project Cost (in millions)

- ◯ <5M
- ◯ 5-9M
- ◯ 10-14M
- ◯ 15-19M
- ◯ 20-24M
- ◯ 25-29M
- ◯ 30-34M
- ◯ 35-39M
- ◯ 40-44M
- ◯ 45-49M
- ◯ 50-54M
- ◯ 55-59M
- ◯ 60-64M
- ◯ 65-69M
- ◯ 70-74M
- ◯ 75-79M
- ◯ 80-99M
- ◯ 100M+

6. In what year(s) was this building completed and occupied?

Completed ____________________

Occupied ____________________

Planning

Survey of New Academic Library Buildings 2003-2009

Responses in this section will be used to determine planning factors for new academic library buildings completed since 2003. Question #7 is used with permission from the Council on Library and Information Resources.

7. Which of the following considerations motivated your library building project? Please indicate the strength of motivation for as many considerations that apply. Use the last column to indicate the consideration was not a factor.

	Strong Motivation		Intermediate Motivation		Weak Motivation	N/A
Growth of library staff (either librarians or support staff)	○	○	○	○	○	○
Increase in number of library service points	○	○	○	○	○	○
Growth of the collections	○	○	○	○	○	○
Changing character of student body space needs	○	○	○	○	○	○
Change in reference services	○	○	○	○	○	○
Changes in public services other than circulation (e.g., ILL)	○	○	○	○	○	○
Changes in information technology	○	○	○	○	○	○
Changes in technical services and other library operations with little interactions with library users	○	○	○	○	○	○
Preservation of the collections	○	○	○	○	○	○
Need to accommodate operations not previously housed in the library (e.g., computing centers; general classrooms or offices)	○	○	○	○	○	○
Aesthetic considerations and creature comfort	○	○	○	○	○	○
Building safety issues	○	○	○	○	○	○
Mechanical systems obsolescence	○	○	○	○	○	○
Requirements of the Americans	○	○	○	○	○	○

with Disabilities Act

Building structural problems (including earthquake protection) ○ ○ ○ ○ ○ ○

Dysfunctional design of previous space ○ ○ ○ ○ ○ ○

Other considerations (please describe)

8. Was LEED (Leadership in Energy & Environmental Design) or other considerations for environmental sustainability factored into the new library's design and construction?

○ Yes

○ No

If yes, please briefly describe

9. What were the sources of funding for this project? (check all that apply)

☐ Capital campaign (if yes, please indicate whether this was part of a broader institutional campaign or a campaign only for the new library)

☐ Part of institutional campaign

☐ Library-only campaign

☐ State/government funding

☐ College or university regular capital budget

Other (please describe)

Survey of New Academic Library Buildings 2003-2009

10. How old was the facility the new building replaced?

- ◯ <25 years
- ◯ 100+ years
- ◯ 25-49 years
- ◯ 50-74 years
- ◯ 75-99 years
- ◯ The new building is an addition (skip to question 12)

11. Was the old building demolished?

- ◯ Yes
- ◯ No

If no, what is the old building being used for now?

New Building Characteristics

Responses in this section will be used to identify specific characteristics of the new academic library space. Responses may be left blank if data is unavailable.

12. Is the new building larger than the old building?

- ◯ Yes
- ◯ No

13. Please indicate the approximate size of the new building.

- ◯ Less than 50,000 square feet
- ◯ 50,000 to 74,999 square feet
- ◯ 75,000 to 99,999 square feet
- ◯ 100,000 to 149,000 square feet
- ◯ 150,000 to 199,999 square feet
- ◯ 200,000 to 299,999 square feet
- ◯ 300,000 or more square feet

14. Please indicate the percentage of the new building designated for library purposes.

- ◯ Less than 50%
- ◯ 50% - 74%
- ◯ 75% - 99%
- ◯ 100%

15. Compared to the old facility, how many public access computers are located in the new building?

- ◯ More
- ◯ Less
- ◯ Approximately the same

Survey of New Academic Library Buildings 2003-2009

16. Approximately how many public access computers are located in the new building?

- ○ <25
- ○ 25-49
- ○ 50-99
- ○ 100-149
- ○ 150-199
- ○ 200-299
- ○ 300-399
- ○ 400+

17. Was increasing the number of electrical outlets available for patron use an important design consideration in the new facility?

- ○ Yes
- ○ No

18. How does the number of general use seats in the new facility compare with the old facility?

- ○ There are more general use seats in the new building
- ○ There are fewer general use seats in the new building
- ○ The number of general use seats has not changed significantly

Survey of New Academic Library Buildings 2003-2009

19. Approximately how many general use seats are available in the new building?

- Less than 100
- 100-499
- 500-999
- 1000-1499
- 1500-1999
- 2000+

20. Compared to the old facility, how much soft seating (lounges, couches) is available in the new building?

- There is significantly more soft seating available in the new building
- There amount of soft seating has not changed significantly
- There is less soft seating available in the new building

21. How does the number of group study rooms in the new building compare with the old facility?

- There are significantly more (50%+) group study rooms available in the new building
- There are more group study rooms available in the new building
- The number of group study rooms is about the same
- There are fewer group study rooms available in the new building

Survey of New Academic Library Buildings 2003-2009

22. How many group study rooms are available in the new facility?

- ◯ None
- ◯ 1-5
- ◯ 6-10
- ◯ 11-19
- ◯ 20-29
- ◯ 30+

23. Compared to the old facility, how much space in the new building has been designated for quiet study?

- ◯ There is more space designated for quiet study in the new building
- ◯ The amount of space designated for quiet study has remained about the same
- ◯ There is less space designated for quiet study in the new building
- ◯ This library does does not designate specific areas for quiet study

24. Compared to the old facility, are there more or fewer faculty carrels in the new facility? Select all that apply.

- ☐ The number of faculty carrels has increased
- ☐ The number of faculty carrels has decreased
- ☐ The number of faculty carrels has remained about the same
- ☐ There were no faculty carrels in the old building
- ☐ There are no faculty carrels in the new building

Survey of New Academic Library Buildings 2003-2009

25. Compared to the old facility, has the number of classrooms and/or computer labs designated primarily for library use only increased?

- ◯ The number of library classrooms has increased
- ◯ The number of library classrooms has remained the same
- ◯ There are fewer library classrooms in the new building

26. How many library classrooms are available in the new facility?

- ◯ None
- ◯ 1-2
- ◯ 3-5
- ◯ 6-9
- ◯ 10-14
- ◯ 15+

27. Compared to the old facility, has the amount of space for library staff (offices, conference rooms, etc.) increased?

- ◯ The amount of space for library staff has increased
- ◯ The amount of space for library staff has remained the same
- ◯ The amount of space for library staff has decreased

28. Compared to the old facility, has the number of service points increased in the new facility?

- ◯ There are more public service points in the new facility
- ◯ The number of public service points has remained the same
- ◯ The are fewer public service points in the new facilty

Survey of New Academic Library Buildings 2003-2009

29. What percentage of the public areas in the new facility have wireless network access?

- ◯ Less than 25%
- ◯ 25-49%
- ◯ 50-74%
- ◯ 75-99%
- ◯ 100%

30. Compared to the old facility, have hours of operation increased in the new building?

- ◯ Hours of operation have increased
- ◯ Hours of operation have remained the same
- ◯ Hours of operation have decreased

31. Do you offer 24 hour access to the new building?

- ◯ Yes
- ◯ No

32. If you answered yes to the previous question, please describe. Select all that apply.

- ☐ 24 hour access during finals and/or reading weeks
- ☐ 24 hour access during academic terms
- ☐ 24 hour access to limited sections of building
- ☐ 24 hour access to entire facility

Other (describe)

Survey of New Academic Library Buildings 2003-2009

33. Please list 2-3 spaces in the new building you think best represent the library's role in academic life on your campus.

1.
2.
3.

34. Please list 2-3 spaces in the library you think best represent the role of the library in other aspects of campus life (e.g., social, cultural).

1.
2.
3.

35. Please describe your library's food and drink policy.

- ☐ Food and beverages permitted
- ☐ Food and beverages prohibited
- ☐ Food prohibited but beverages allowed
- ☐ Only covered beverages allowed

Other (please describe)

Non-library Facilities

Responses in this section will be used to describe the inclusion of non-library facilities and provide more detailed information on multi-use in the new library space.

Survey of New Academic Library Buildings 2003-2009

36. Please select what types of non-library facilities are/were located in the old and new buildings. Please select all that apply.

	Old facility	New facility
General computer lab(s)	☐	☐
Snack bar or cafe	☐	☐
General use classrooms	☐	☐
Conference/meeting rooms	☐	☐
Auditorium	☐	☐
Tutoring center	☐	☐
Writing center	☐	☐
Archives	☐	☐
Bookstore	☐	☐
Copy center	☐	☐
Academic department(s)	☐	☐
Art gallery or museum space	☐	☐

Other (please describe)

Collection Variables

Responses in this section will be used to identify patterns and describe the relationship between physical collections and the new academic library space. Responses may be left blank if data is unavailable.

37. Using the NCES definition below, how many physical volumes are in this library's collection?

Definition: Total number of volumes (as defined below) of books, serial backfiles, and other paper materials held at the end of the fiscal year.

Includes duplicate and bound volumes of periodicals. For the purposes of this survey, unclassified bound serials arranged in alphabetical order are considered classified. Excludes microfilms, maps, nonprint materials, and uncataloged items. Includes government document volumes that are accessible through the library's catalogs regardless of whether or not they are separately shelved. "Classified" includes documents arranged by Superintendent of Documents, CODOC, or similar numbers. "Cataloged" includes documents for which records are provided by the library or downloaded from other sources into the library's card or online catalogs. Documents should, to the extent possible, be counted as they would if they were in bound volumes (e.g., 12 issues of an annual serial would be one or two volumes). Title and piece counts are not considered the same.

- ◯ Less than 50,000
- ◯ 50,000-99,000
- ◯ 100,000-249,999
- ◯ 250,000-499,000
- ◯ 500,000-999,000
- ◯ 1,000,000-2,999,999
- ◯ 2,000,000-3,999,999
- ◯ 4,000,000-5,999,999
- ◯ More than 6,000,000

Survey of New Academic Library Buildings 2003-2009

38. What percentage of these are in open stacks?

- ◯ Less than 50%
- ◯ 50%-74%
- ◯ 75%-90%
- ◯ 91%-100%

39. How would you describe the rate of growth of the print collection?

- ◯ Number of volumes added is increasing each year
- ◯ Number of volumes added each year remains static
- ◯ Number of volumes added each year is declining

40. Does this library have compact shelving?

- ◯ Yes
- ◯ No

41. If you answered yes to the previous question, what percentage of the collection is stored in compact shelving?

- ◯ Less than 10%
- ◯ 10%-24%
- ◯ 25%-49%
- ◯ 50%-74%
- ◯ 75%-99%
- ◯ 100%

Survey of New Academic Library Buildings 2003-2009

42. Does this library have an automated storage and retrieval system?

- ◯ Yes
- ◯ No

43. If you answered yes to the previous question, what percentage of the collection is retrievable via the automated storage and retrieval system?

- ◯ Less than 10%
- ◯ 10%-24%
- ◯ 25%-49%
- ◯ 50%-74%
- ◯ 75%-99%
- ◯ 100%

44. Does the library have an off-site storage facility?

- ◯ Yes
- ◯ No

45. If you answered yes to the previous question, what percentage of the collection is housed in off-site storage?

- ◯ None
- ◯ Less than 10%
- ◯ 10%-24%
- ◯ 25%-49%
- ◯ 50%-99%
- ◯ 100%

Survey of New Academic Library Buildings 2003-2009

46. Given this library's rate of print collection growth, at what point in the future would you estimate that its shelving capacity for print materials will be exhausted?

- ○ 2009-10
- ○ 2011-15
- ○ 2016-20
- ○ 2021-25
- ○ 2026-30
- ○ 2031 or later

47. Please list the three most important factors that will affect planning for this library's print collections in the coming years.

1. ______
2. ______
3. ______

Usage Data

Data in this section will be used to determine usage patterns for new academic library buildings. Data from this section will also be linked to specific building features to determine relationships between these attributes and facility usage. Responses may be left blank if data are unavailable.

48. Using data from your library's annual data report, please describe usage levels in the new facility as measured in exit gate counts.

- ◯ Use of the new facility has increased significantly (25%-100%) compared to the old facility
- ◯ Use of the new facility has increased moderately (10%-24%) compared to the old facility
- ◯ Use of the new facility has increased marginally (<10%) compared to the old facility
- ◯ Use of the new facility is about the same in the new facility as the old facility
- ◯ Use of the new facility has declined when compared to the old facility

49. If this information is readily available to you, please provide exit gate counts for the last full, pre-construction year in the old facility and the latest full year in the new facility.

Last full year in old facility

Latest full year in new facility

50. Compared to the latest year's gate count, what do you expect next year's final gate count to be?

- ◯ More (1-10%) than last year
- ◯ Somewhat more (10-25%)than last year
- ◯ Significantly more (>25%) than last year
- ◯ About the same as last year
- ◯ Less (<10%) than last year
- ◯ Somewhat less (10%-25%) than last year
- ◯ Significantly less (<25%) than last year

51. What do you consider to be the most important facility usage measurements for this library in order of importance?

1.

2.

3.

Survey of New Academic Library Buildings 2003-2009

52. Based on your observations, what are the three busiest areas in this new facility?

1.
2.
3.

53. Has there been any aspect of usage of the new facility that you did not expect? If so, please describe.

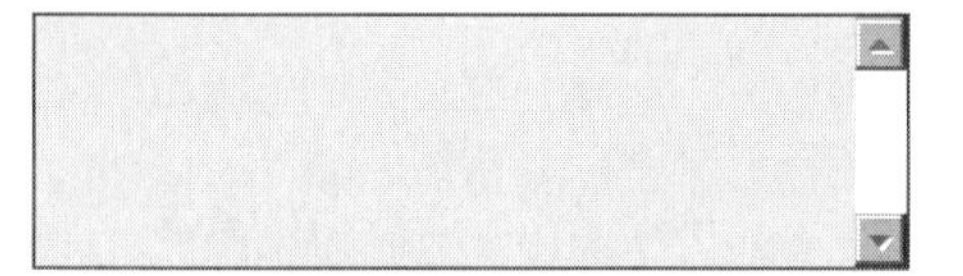

REFERENCES

2008 Library design showcase. (2008). *American Libraries, 39*(4), 44–57.

2009 Library design showcase. (2009). *American Libraries,* 40(4), 30-42.

2009 Library design showcase digital supplement. (2009). Retrieved January 15, 2010, from http://americanlibraries-magazine.org/archives/digital-supplement/spring-2009

Academics | The University of Chicago (n.d.). Retrieved March 28, 2010, from http://www.uchicago.edu/academics/index.shtml

Albanese, A. R. (2003). Deserted no more. *Library Journal, 28*(7), 34–36.

Albanese, A. R. (2006). Breaking ground. *Library Journal, 131,* 1–7.

Antell, K., & Engel, D. (2006). Conduciveness to scholarship: The essence of academic library as place. *College & Research Libraries, 67*(6), 536–560.

Atkins, S. E. (1991). *The academic library and the American university.* Chicago: American Library Association.

Bahr, A. H. (2000). Library buildings in a digital age, why bother? *College & Research Libraries News, 61*(7), 590.

Bazillion, R. J. (2001). The wisdom of hindsight: A new library one year later. *American Libraries,* 32(4), 72.

Bazillion, R. J., & Braun, C. L. (2001). *Academic libraries as high-tech gateways: A guide.* Chicago: American Library Association.

Beagle, D. (1999). Conceptualizing an information commons. *The Journal of Academic Librarianship,* 25(2), 82–89.

Bennett, C. (2007). A new story to tell: The east commons at the Georgia Tech Library. *Georgia Library Quarterly,* 43(4), 17–18.

Bennet, S. (2003). *Libraries designed for learning.* Washington, DC: Council on Library and Information Resources.

Bennet, S. (2005). Righting the balance. *Library as place: Rethinking roles, rethinking space* (pp. 10–24). Washington, DC: Council on Library and Information Resources.

Bennett, S. (2007). First questions for designing higher education learning spaces. *The Journal of Academic Librarianship,* 33(1), 14–26.

The boom goes on: A facilities showcase. (1999). *American Libraries, 30*(4), 52.

Boone, M. D. (2002). Library design—the architect's view. A discussion with Tom Findley. *Library Hi Tech, 20*(3), 388–392.

Building for the future. (2003). *American Libraries,* 34(4), 40.

Building on the past. (2004). *American Libraries,* 35(4), 38–58.

Burr Oliver, K. (2005). The Johns Hopkins Medical Library as base: Information professionals working in library user environments. (pp. 66–75). Washington, DC: Council on Library and Information Resources.

Carnegie Foundation. (n.d.) *The Carnegie classification of institutions of higher education.* Retrieved October 30, 2008, from http://www.carnegiefoundation.org

Carlson, S. (2001). The deserted library: As students work online, reading rooms empty out leading some campuses to add Starbucks. *Chronicle of Higher Education, 48*(12), A35–A38.

Chism, N. V. N. (2006). Challenging traditional assumptions and rethinking learning spaces. *Learning spaces* (pp. 1–12) Educause. Retrieved November 21, 2008, from http://net.educause.edu/ir/library/pdf/PUB7102b.pdf

The Chronicle of Higher Education. (2008). *Campus architecture*. Retrieved December 19, 2008, from http://chronicle.com/stats/architecture/index.php

Crawford, W. (1998). Paper persists: Why physical library collections still matter. *Online, 22*(1), 42.

Crawford, W. (1999). Library space. *Online, 23*(2), 61.

Crawford, W., & Gorman, M. (1995). *Future libraries: Dreams, madness, and reality*. Chicago: American Library Association.

Creswell, J. W. (2008). *Educational research: Planning, conducting, and evaluating quantitative and qualitative research*. Upper Saddle River, NJ: Pearson/Merrill/Prentice Hall.

Crosbie, J. W., & Hickey, D. D. (2001). *When change is set in stone: An analysis of seven academic libraries designed by Perry Dean Rogers & Partners*. Chicago: American Library Association.

Demas, S. (2005). From the Ashes of Alexandria: What's Happening in the College Library? *Library as place: Rethinking roles, rethinking space* (pp. 25–40). Washington, DC: Council on Library and Information Resources.

Demas, S., & Scherer, J. A. (2002). Esprit de place. *American Libraries, 33*(4), 65.

Dilevko, J., & Gottlieb, L. (2002). Print sources in an electronic age: A vital part of the research process for undergraduate students. *The Journal of Academic Librarianship, 28*(6), 381–392.

Dillon, A. (2008). Accelerating learning and discovery: redefining the role of the academic librarian. In *No Brief Candle: Reconceiving Research Libraries for the 21st Century* (pp. 51-57). Washington, D.C.: Council on Library and Information Resources.

Dillon, D. (2004). College libraries: The long goodbye. *Chronicle of Higher Education, 51*(16), B5–B5.

Dougherty, R. M., & Adams, M. (2001). Campus libraries: Time to market an undervalued asset? *Library Issues, 22*(2), 1–4.

Dove, A. (2004). Designing space for knowledge work. *Library & Information Update, 3*(3), 22–24.

Dowler, L. (1996). Our edifice at the precipice. *Library Journal, 121*(3), 118.

Dreazen, E. (1999). Honoring advances in architecture: The AIA/ALA buildings awards. *American Libraries, 30*(4), 70.

Equity by design. (2007). *American Libraries, 38*(4), 34–48.

Engel, D., & Antell, K. (2004). The life of the mind: A study of faculty spaces in academic libraries. *College & Research Libraries, 65*(1), 8–26.

Facilities showcase. (1998). *American Libraries, 29*(4), 66.

Facilities Showcase: So goes the community. (2005). *American Libraries, 36*(4), 32–51.

Finnerty, C. (2002). Library planning in the electronic era: Are the stacks necessary? *Information Outlook, 6*(8), 6–8.

Foote, S. M. (2004). Charges in library design: Architect's perspective. *Portal: Libraries & the Academy, 4*(1), 41–59.

Foundations of knowledge. (2001). *American Libraries, 32*(4), 44.

Fox, B. (1999). Structural ergonomics. *Library Journal, 124*(20), 57.

Fox, B. (2000a). Library buildings, 1999: Structural ergonomics. In D. Bogart (Ed.), *The Bowker annual library and book trade almanac* (45th ed., pp. 453–466). Medford, NJ: Information Today.

Fox, B. (2000b). Strength in numbers. *Library Journal, 125*(20), 50.

Fox, B. (2001). Library buildings 2000: Strength in numbers. In D. Bogart (Ed.), *The Bowker annual library and book trade almanac* (46th ed.). Medford, NJ: Information Today.

Fox, B. (2002a). The building buck doesn't stop here. *Library Journal, 127*(20), 42–54.

Fox, B. (2002b). Library buildings 2001: Keep on constructin'. In D. Bogart (Ed.), *The Bowker annual library and book trade almanac* (47th ed., pp. 468–491). Medford, NJ: Information Today.

Fox, B. (Ed.). (2003a). *Library buildings 2002: The building buck doesn't stop here* (48th ed.). Medford, NJ: Information Today.

Fox, B. (2003b). These joints are jumpin'. *Library Journal, 128*(20), 36–49.

Fox, B. (2004a). Research and statistics, library buildings 2003: These joints are jumpin'. In D. Bogart (Ed.) *The Bowker annual 2004: Library and book trade almanac* (49th ed., pp. 462–465). Medford, NJ: Information Today.

Fox, B. (2004b). Spend billions and they will come. *Library Journal, 129*(20), 48–61.

Fox, B. (2005a). Research and statistics, library buildings 2004: Projects top $1.2 billion nationally. In D. Bogart (Ed.), *The Bowker annual 2005: Library and book trade almanac* (50th ed., pp. 486–489). Medford, NJ: Information Today.

Fox, B. (2005b). A storm rains on our parade. *Library Journal, 130*(20), 44–58.

Fox, B. (2006a). Betwixt and be teen. *Library Journal, 131*(20), 42–56.

Fox, B. (2006b). Research and statistics, library buildings 2005: A storm rains on our parade. In D. Bogart (Ed.), *The Bowker annual 2006: Library and book trade almanac* (51st ed., pp. 483–485). Medford, NJ: Information Today.

Fox, B. (2007a). Going, going, green. *Library Journal, 132*(20), 44–55.

Fox, B. (2007b). Research and statistics, library buildings 2006: Betwixt and be teen. In D. Bogart (Ed.), *The Bowker annual 2007: Library and book trade almanac* (52nd ed., pp. 426–428). Medford, NJ: Information Today.

Fox, B. (2008a). Library buildings 2008: Keeping the "eco" in economy. *Library Journal, 133*(20), 36–39.

Fox, B. (2009). The constant library. *Library Journal,* 134(20), 26-40.

Fox, B. (2008b). Research and statistics, library buildings 2007: Going, going, green. In D. Bogart (Ed.), *The Bowker annual 2008: Library and book trade almanac* (53rd ed., pp. 492–494). Medford, NJ: Information Today.

Fox, B., & Cassin, E. (1996). Beating the high cost of libraries. *Library Journal, 121*(20), 43–55.

Fox, B., & Jones, E. J. (1998). Another year, another $543 million. *Library Journal, 123*(20), 41.

Fox, B., & Jones, E. J. (1999). Library buildings, 1998: Another year, another $543 million. In D. Bogart (Ed.), *The Bowker annual library and book trade almanac* (44th ed., pp. 489–502). Medford, NJ: Information Today.

Fox, B., & Kremen, M. L. (1998). Library buildings, 1997: The renovation role model. In D. Bogart (Ed.), *The Bowker annual library and book trade almanac* (43rd ed., pp. 457–475). Medford, NJ: Information Today.

Freeman, G. T. (2005). The library as place: Changes in learning pattern, collections, technology, and use. *Library as place: Rethinking roles, rethinking space* (pp. 1–9). Washington, DC: Council on Library and Information Resources.

Frischer, B. (2005). The ultimate Internet cafe: Reflections of a practicing digital humanist about designing a future for the research library. *Library as place: Rethinking roles, rethinking space* (pp. 41–55). Washington, DC: Council on Library and Information Resources.

Gaspari-Bridges, P. (2008). The Lewis Science Library. *Friends of the Princeton University Library Newsletter,* Spring 2008(26), 1.

Gosling, W. A. (2000). To go or not to go? Library as place. *American Libraries, 31*(11), 44.

Hardesty, L. (2000). *Do we need academic libraries?* Chicago: Association of College and Research Libraries.

Harrington, D. (2001). Six trends in library design. *Library Journal, 126*(20), 12.

Hiller, S. (2004). Measure by measure: Assessing the viability of the physical library. *The Bottom Line: Managing Library Finances, 17*(4), 126–131.

Informational services for instructors. (2008). Retrieved December 4, 2008, from http://www.lib.purdue.edu/rguides/instructionalservices/

Kaufman, P. (2001). Whose good old days are these? A dozen predictions for the digital age. *Journal of Library Administration, 35*(3), 5.

King, H. (2000). *The academic library in the 21st century—what need for a physical place?* Paper presented at the International Association of Technology University Libraries Annual Conference 2000. Retrieved May 12, 2008, from http://www.iatul.org/doclibrary/public/Conf_Proceedings/2000/King.rtf

Kohl, D. F. (2004). From the editor... the paperless society... not quite yet. *Journal of Academic Librarianship, 30*(3), 177–178.

Lewis, D. W. (2007). A strategy for academic libraries in the first quarter of the 21st century. *College & Research Libraries, 68*(5), 418–434.

Libraries = cultural icons: 2006 showcase of new and renovated facilities. (2006). *American Libraries, 37*(4), 28–47.

Lombardi, M., & Wall, T. B. (2006). Duke University: Perkins Library. *Learning spaces* (pp. 1–10) Educause. Retrieved November 22, 2008, from http://net.educause.edu/ir/library/pdf/P7102cs4.pdf

MacWhinnie, L. A. (2003). The information commons: The academic library of the future. *Portal: Libraries & the Academy, 3*(2), 241.

Mann, T. (2001). The importance of books, free access, and libraries as places—and the dangerous inadequacy of the information science paradigm. *The Journal of Academic Librarianship, 27*(4), 268–281.

Martell, C. (2001). The ubiquitous user: A reexamination of Carlson's deserted library. *Portal: Libraries & the Academy, 5*(4), 441–453.

Martell, C. (2007). The elusive user: Changing use patterns in academic libraries 1995 to 2004. *College & Research Libraries, 68*(5), 435–444.

McDonald, A. (2002). Planning the virtual library: A virtual impossibility? *Serials, 15*(3), 237–244.

Michalak, S. (1994). Planning academic library facilities: The library will have walls. *Journal of Library Administration, 20*(2), 93–113.

Mighty Multnomah and other fabulous facilities. (1997). *American Libraries, 28*(4), 38.

Monahan, T. (2002). Flexible space & built pedagogy: Emerging IT embodiments. *Inventio, 4*(1), 1–19.

Morrow, J. B. (2008). Prices of U.S. and foreign published materials. In D. Bogart (Ed.), *The Bowker annual book trade almanac* (43rd ed., pp. 513–534). Medford, NJ: Information Today.

Newman, F., Courturier, L., & Scurry, J. (2004). Autonomy, accountability, and the new compact. *The futures project: Policy for higher education in a changing world* (pp. 104–134). San Francisco: Jossey Bass.

Patton, M. Q. (2002). *Qualitative research & evaluation methods* (3rd ed.). Thousand Oaks, CA: Sage.

Peterson, C. A. (2005). Space designed for lifelong learning: The Dr. Martin Luther King Jr. Joint-Use Library. *Library as place: Rethinking roles, rethinking space* (pp. 56–65). Washington, DC: Council on Library and Information Resources.

Potter, W. G. (2004). *The library as place: The student learning center at the University of Georgia.*, Retrieved May 21, 2008, from http://web.cni.org/tfms/2004a.spring/handouts/Spring2004handouts/cni_brief_on_slc.doc

Ranseen, E. (2002). The library as place: Changing perspectives. *Library Administration & Management, 16*(4), 203–207.

Rizzo, J. C. (2002). Finding your place in the information age library. *New Library World, 103*(1182/1183), 457–456.

Salkind, N. J. (2008). *Statistics for people who (think they) hate statistics.* Thousand Oaks, CA: Sage.

Sannwald, W. W. (2001a). *Checklist of library building design considerations* (4th ed.). Chicago: American Library Association.

Sannwald, W. W. (2001b). To build or not to build. *Library Administration & Management, 15*(3), 155–160.

Schonwald, J. (2005, June 5). University to expand library collections to prepare next generation of scholars. *University of Chicago Chronicle.* Retrieved May 16, 2008, from http://chronicle.uchicago.edu

Schooldesigns.com. (2008). Retrieved December 28, 2008, from http://www.schooldesigns.com/

Seeds, R. S. (2002). Impact of a digital archive (JSTOR) on print collection use. *Collection Building, 21*(3), 120–122.

A sense of place. (2002). *American Libraries, 33*(4), 44–60.

Shill, H. B., & Tonner, S. (2003). Creating a better place: Physical improvements in academic libraries, 1995–2002. *College & Research Libraries, 64*(6), 431–466.

Shill, H. B., & Tonner, S. (2004). Does the building still matter? Usage patterns in new, expanded, and renovated libraries, 1995–2002. *College & Research Libraries, 65*(2), 123–150.

Thomas, M. A. (2000). Redefining the library space: Managing the coexistence of books, computers, and readers. *Journal of Academic Librarianship, 26*(6), 408–415.

Values set in steel. (2000). *American Libraries, 31*(4), 50.

Wakaruk, A. (2009). Disconnecting the disconnect: Thinking about public space in academic libraries. *College & Research Libraries News, 70*(1), 16–19.

Walters, W. H. (2009). Journal prices, book acquisitions, and sustainable college library collections. *College & Research Libraries, 69*(6), 576–586.

Weise, F. (2004). Being there: Library as place. *Journal of the Medical Library Association, 91*(1), 6–13.

Wilson, L. A. (2003). If we build it, will they come? Library users in a digital world. *Journal of Library Administration, 39*(4), 19–28.

ABOUT THE AUTHOR

Dr. Christopher Stewart is Dean of Libraries at Illinois Institute of Technology and a member of the adjunct faculty of the Graduate School of Library & Information Science at Dominican University. His research interests include the evolving library physical space, organizational change, and the role of academic libraries in higher education reform. Dr. Stewart has an MLIS from Dominican University, an MBA from Illinois Institute of Technology, and a doctorate in higher education management from the University of Pennsylvania, where his dissertation focused on emerging trends in academic library building planning and design.